GRACE AND THE SEARCHING
OF OUR HEART

*"O Lord, thou hast searched
me and known me!"*
Psalm 139:1

Grace and

the Searching
of Our Heart

By CHARLES R. STINNETTE, Jr.

New York : Association Press

Preface

IN PSALM 145:18 we are assured that the Lord is near unto all who call upon him *faithfully*. It is that last word which frequently escapes our attention. The trouble with most petitions is that we as askers want a job done *without getting personally involved*. Like the seekers after magic in every age we look for a wizard and quick accomplishment, not enduring faithfulness—in ourselves or in God. It is not surprising, then, that the pain of self-discovery comes as a shock. It strikes us first like "the pains of hell" and "the snares of death."

The mystery of grace is that God precedes us both in pain and in its resolution. The shock of recognition, in the light of grace, is but the first note of the symphony of God's recovery of his own. Our faithfulness in calling upon that grace is not grounded in our steadfastness, but in his. The New Testament reminds us that if our hearts condemn us, God is greater than our hearts. It is his love—his grace—which precedes the searching of our hearts.

This book is intended for those who have undertaken the task of self-discovery. Socrates' dictum that an unexamined life is not worth living has become an im-

v

perative in this day of agonizing reappraisal. Man's quest to discover who he is springs from deeper sources than psychological dilettantism. Parents and children, teachers and students, workers and thoughtful inquirers, and those upon whom life has imposed self-examination as a necessity will, we hope, find this companion-in-faith helpful.

It is with gratitude that I record here my appreciation to my wife for her help at every stage in the development of this book.

CHARLES R. STINNETTE, JR.
Union Theological Seminary

Contents

Introduction

THE ACT OF FAITH—simply as a phenomenon of life—is the crucible in which the self is formed. In faith one gathers himself with an integrity which transcends the many faces of his personage. The child who announces proudly, "Today, I climbed the jungle-gym, Daddy!" is both proclaiming his identity and affirming the stability of his selfhood in action. His declaration is rooted in present fact and in a firm prospect for his future action as a person. Kierkegaard, it may be remembered, held that faith is the means of self-actualization. He wrote, "Faith is: that the self in being itself and in willing to be itself is grounded transparently in God." * [1]

But it is just here in the relation of faith to our selfhood, in this willingness to be ourselves as grounded transparently in God, that we have fallen upon barren times. Our most poignant failures are failures of will. Try as we will we cannot find ourselves in the sight of God. If we have not lost our selves we have surely misplaced our identity somewhere in this pilgrimage of

---

* Numbered references are found at the end of the Introduction and of each chapter, except those belonging to the half titles for the four parts of the book.

9

life. How then shall we give that which we no longer possess? Have we become alien to the promises of God, no longer remembering that occasion of faith when fear was transfigured by a great joy and all men knew themselves to be in Christ?

It is toward a retracing of this "Everyman's journey" in contemporary dress which this companion-in-faith proposes. At the least, maturity involves a disposition toward a recurring opening of oneself to new depths of truth. In this day when psychotherapy and other ventures in self-discovery are preparing the way for such openness, perhaps we need the reminder that acquired sensitiveness, apart from a firm sense of identity, may be an occasion for new fear and conformity rather than for new acts of faith and boldness in love.[2] The saving possibility in every self-discovery is made possible by the courage which comes when deep cries unto deep and one knows again that his first citizenship and charter of freedom are expressed in the words, "God created man in his own image." At heart man *knows* that he was not intended for fear but for sonship. If our humanity is rooted in our relationship to God who— ourselves included—can be against us?

Biblical religion is concretely concerned with *hearing* and *responding* to the ultimate claims of God upon our lives—claims that appear both as judgment and as gift. At its center there is the affirmation and the fact that God in Christ (to use the arresting phrase of the King James Version), ". . . led captivity captive, and gave gifts unto men." [3] Giving and forgiving, then, are the first modes of biblical revelation. Our matching response—and our problem—is to *hear* this revelation anew as if for the first time.

As companions-in-faith we suggest that in the light of this first responsibility for hearing, we adopt two rules which shall govern our attitude in this quest:

First, that the change which we hope for will come not so much by trying harder but by looking closer. To look closer is to hear and to comprehend more adequately what actually exists. It is to know ourselves and others in the actuality of concrete existence.

Second, to look closer and to hear more deeply is by its very mode an action that is prior to trying harder. It is to turn, since repentance (*metanonia*) is a turning. Too much religious activity amounts to heavy burdens imposed upon those whose eyes and ears and hearts remain unmoved. The *Prayer Book* rendering of a recurring phrase in Psalm 80 puts the sequence of change in its biblical mode: "Turn us again, O God; show the light of thy countenance, and we shall be whole." To turn and to behold again ourselves and our neighbors in the light of God's revelation is to begin an action which depends not so much upon our own effort as upon the power of grace to create a new thing out of nothingness.

I. THE SHOCK OF RECOGNITION

If hearing is our first task, the pilgrimage begins with a prayer that the word of truth may be heard in all its heart-piercing judgment, which only grace can endure. The truth comes upon us as the shock of recognition. All learning involves something of the shock of reality—

just as responsible change begins in dissatisfaction. But the truth of revelation bears a surgical objectivity which lays open the wound in man's soul. It not only locates the pain but it also exposes the pathology behind the pain.

To know oneself or to know another is to behold "fear in a handful of dust," as T. S. Eliot has phrased it. Man is afraid of death but even more afraid of life. He fears its pitiless revelation of emptiness in the wake of the demand for creative response, and its insistence that a man discover who he is. These are shocks which macerate the human heart. But they point to the deeper shock of recognition, namely, that man's pain is a reminder of his vocation under God. His faithless fear then is evidence that he has already abandoned his birthright as a man. The motto of Huxley's *Brave New World* is in some measure a demonstration of the reaction to shock in modern man. One could hardly find more immediate documentation that the passion of twentieth-century man is not freedom but conformity and its consequent retreat from humanity. The slogan, "community, identity, and stability" holds an appeal only for those who have forgotten that no community is worth saving unless it is willing to die for the truth, that there is no identity except in diversity and no stability save in openness to change.

The shock of recognition fulfills its proper function when in recalling us to ourselves it prepares us for that openness to change. The religious attitude which conveys this openness to change is contrition. The work of grace in searching our heart is directed toward the transformation of a broken spirit into a contrite heart.

In the first section of the pilgrimage which we are about to undertake we shall explore some of the ways in which the shock of recognition comes upon us.

The contemporary experience is marked by rapid change, routinized technology, and the growing loneliness of the individual lost in the mass. In such a world it is not surprising that man increasingly pictures himself as the victim of forces beyond his control. Indeed, he can achieve a high degree of rationality about his helplessness—along with an amazing credulousness for superstition in expecting relief from magic forces, also beyond him. The unexpected discovery in all this quite reasonable mood of helplessness is that in renouncing responsibility as illusion we have renounced the person! It is in this setting that we may hear again, "Let us make man in our image, after our likeness; and let them have dominion. . . ."[4]

II. THE TRINITY AND THE ROOTS OF OUR IDENTITY

It is precisely because man is the bearer of an infinite intention that he can never become merely the pawn of alien forces. As Pascal said, man remains the creature who can take compass: "We are something and we are not everything."[5] Unfortunately this assurance does not settle the matter for the man who lives in a technological world. If human behavior is not entirely determined by impersonal forces our only alternative appears to be a return to the capriciousness of an erratic deity. How is it possible that man, made in the image of God and exercising dominion under God, may be anything but a puppet? It is in answer to this question that the trinity as the mode of heaven may be seen as bearing a relation to the roots of man's identity.

It was Luther who insisted that because man is the most free of all creatures by virtue of his relation to God's grace in faith, man is also the most willing servant of all in gratitude and thanksgiving. Here the mode of God's gift is crucial in shaping the manner of man's response.

The trinity as a doctrine in Christian history has served to affirm the unity of God within the diversity of his modes. We do not propose to explicate a full trinitarian metaphysic but rather to emphasize that we may know and serve God (and thus come to know and to realize our own identity) in the manner and through the means which he has employed to reveal himself to us. Man's identity is ontologically rooted in the social and incarnational mode of God as Creator, Redeemer, and in-dwelling Holy Spirit. This is the economy of God mediated through the Holy Trinity which remains as a summary of the basic creedal affirmation of the Christian faith to this day.

In a world of technology it becomes increasingly necessary to answer the question of how the implicit power of faith becomes explicit in man's life. If we really accept the mode of revelation as integral to its message the answer has been given in the action of God. We are persons after the mode of heaven, and our identity is rooted in the being of God known to us in his action. Being and acting cannot be separated for the same reason that truth is always truth *as known*. In our creedal affirmation of the trinity we are responding in

like manner to the unity of person, truth, and community in the mode of heaven. F. D. Maurice once pointed
out that the creedal statement begins with a personal
affirmation, "I believe," and it refers not to a scheme of
divinity but to a name, that is, Father, Son, and Holy
Ghost "who has established a holy universal church,
who makes men in a communion of saints, who is the
witness of power whereby they receive forgiveness of
sins, who shall quicken their mortal bodies, who enables them to receive everlasting life." [6]

It is here in our recovered participation in the action
of God that we also begin to rediscover the roots of our
identity. It is quite literally true that man is what he
remembers. Every self-recovery involves remembrance
(anamnesis) as well as an act of faith. The classical
analogy of being as well as the analogy of faith (Barth)
and the analogy of relation (Brunner) are all efforts to
express the mode whereby man finds his identity in
God. In the pages which follow we shall be concerned
to emphasize only that whatever the analogy, man's
recovered relation to God is effected in and through his
appropriate response to the action of God. Theology
may employ its varied analogies to describe that relationship, but it is appropriated and made effectual only
in the action of a true and lively faith.

III. THE OCCASIONS OF GIFT GIVING

In one of the climactic scenes of Dante's *Divine
Comedy* the author is led by Beatrice to the seat of
God who is surrounded by the blessed. Here the poet
gazes upon three mirrors each reflecting the one light.

The vision is described by Dante himself: "In the profound and shining being of the deep light appeared to
me three circles, of three colors and one magnitude." [7]
This image, which as Allen Tate has suggested brings
together in a single moment of action the various mean-
ings of God's grace, is also a symbol of the occasions of
gift giving in man. It represents the gift of God which
penetrates all darkness and enables those who behold
it to walk forth while confiding in God's grace. Like the
Pilgrim in John Bunyan's epic we move forward surrounded by many images of reality and of ourselves but
forever informed, illumined, and guided by that single
shaft of light—that one magnitude.

The capacity of one person to help another—the
capacity to receive and to give gifts—is rooted in the
revelation that such gifts are the heart of reality.
Man's beatitude is cradled in those occasions when from
within the disquietudes of his world and its ever-present cruel fact he is able to bind himself again to the
wonder of that gift whereby he came to be. In that one
magnitude "the world is word, expression, news of
God," as Gerard Manley Hopkins wrote. The Hebrews
savored and perpetuated that occasion in their living
remembrance of the moment, "When Israel went forth
from Egypt. . . ." [8] The Christian in Eucharist recalls
the event of Christ in action but extends that response
in every occasion when, like Paul, he finds that the life
he now lives in the flesh is lived "by faith in the son of
God who loved me and gave himself for me." [9]

The power of Christianity rests in the fact that it is
not primarily demand but fulfillment, not so much a
pledge as an actuality, not a plan for the future but a

realized event. Its characteristic invitation is not "Wait and see" but "Enter and behold." It is from within this indicative mood that the Christian is moved to make every occasion one of thanksgiving. As we find ourselves bound by human ties, nurtured in family and community and judged in all our relations to the world we intend to remind ourselves in the pages to follow that we come to these experiences as those who have already received gifts—and are therefore free to give gifts to one another. The philosopher reminds us that the capacity for wonder is the beginning of wisdom. It is in the child's wide-eyed wonder and delight that we see ourselves reflected in the divine image. The child, like the poet, sees the world as if for the first time. Beyond its perpetual perishing and its slow stain the world is restored in such moments. He who "led captivity captive" once again "gives gifts unto men." Here in the occasion when all circles of light are concentrated into *one magnitude* we find the strength as well as the means of making all occasions, occasions of gift giving.

IV. TRANSFIGURING GRACE

The searching of our heart reveals the profound struggles involved in the rediscovery of our identity. Yet through grace we are enabled to claim ourselves again in the occasions of gift giving. We are changed in the radical sense of transfiguration, however, as we enter into the community of faith whose language and liturgy continually reopen us to grace. Like the lepers in the Gospel story [10] we are healed while we go on our way. Every life crisis may be an occasion for self-discovery and renewal. Our deepest need is for a community life and a liturgy relevant to the continuing work of transfiguring grace.

If it is true to its biblical heritage the Christian life is a continual re-enactment of saving history in the light of contemporary history. This is the Hebraic mode of revelation. William Temple has written that the prophets "were largely occupied in reading the lessons of history to the people whose history it was." [11] This reading is also the mode of transfiguring grace. In the book of Deuteronomy (6:1-9 and 20-25) we glimpse something of the concrete methodology for shaping the character of the Hebrew child. The words upon the heart, the sign upon the hands, and the frontlets between the eyes are the means not merely for the telling of history but also for an entering into the transfiguring event, "We were Pharaoh's slaves in Egypt; and the Lord brought us out of Egypt with a mighty hand...." [12]

We are changed not by an idea alone but by a person. Transfiguration is the fruit of a continuing relationship which can be described only in personal terms. Martin Buber in his book on *Moses* [13] makes much of the fact that the Decalogue is not a catechism but the sign of a relationship whose soul is the word, "Thou." One does not come away from personal encounter unchanged. It is recorded that Moses came from his meeting with Yahweh radiantly bright; and in the transfiguration scene Jesus' "raiment was white *and* glistering." [14] The glory of God leaves its mark upon those who behold him. "The sight of God," wrote Bishop Westcott, "is the transfiguration of man."

It is, then, with this understanding of the change

which is wrought within us as we live into grace, that informs our concluding section. In every act of prayer or work or play we are being changed into that likeness —that one magnitude—whose light illumines our day. The Scripture reminds us, "Therefore be careful lest the light in you be darkness." [15]

• *Notes for the Introduction*

1. Sören Kierkegaard, *Sickness unto Death* (New York: Doubleday Anchor), p. 213. Copyright owner, Princeton University Press, 1941.

2. Allen Wheelis, *The Quest for Identity* (New York: W. W. Norton & Co., Inc., 1958), p. 173, writes: "To undertake psychoanalysis in quest of identity is to pursue an illusion. What one achieves is not identity, but a more sensitive awareness of thoughts and feelings."

3. Ephesians 4:8.

4. Genesis 1:26.

5. Blaise Pascal, *Thoughts* (Paris: P. F. Caillert & Son, 1910), p. 68.

6. F. D. Maurice, *The Kingdom of Christ* (New York: E. P. Dutton & Co., 1837), Vol. II, p. 4.

7. Allen Tate, *The Man of Letters in the Modern World* (New York: Meridian Press, 1955), p. 111.

8. Psalm 141:1.

9. Galatians 2:20.

10. Luke 17:15.

11. William Temple, *Nature, Man and God* (London: The Macmillan Co., Ltd., 1934), p. 303.

12. Deuteronomy 6:21.

13. *Moses: The Revelation and the Covenant* (New York: Harper & Brothers, 1958).

14. Luke 9:29 (KJV).

15. Luke 11:35.

PART ONE

The Shock of Recognition

"You must change your life!"
  (The poet, Rilke, upon encountering a piece of ancient
    sculpture) [1]

"You are the man!"
          (Nathan the prophet before David the king) [2]

Not to have known—as most men have not—either the
mountain or the desert is not to have known one's self. Not
to have known one's self is to have known no one and to
have known no one makes it relatively easy to suppose, as
sociology commonly does, that the central problems are the
problems of technology and politics. It makes it possible to
believe that if the world has gone wrong—and seems likely
to go wronger—that is only because production and distribu-
tion are out of balance or the proper exercise of the fran-
chise has not yet been developed; that a different tax
structure or even, God save the mark, the abolition of the
poll tax in Alabama, points the way to Utopia. It is to forget
too easily that the question of the Good Life—both the

---

[1] Rainer Maria Rilke, *Little Treasury of World Poetry*, Hubert
Creekmore, ed. (New York: Charles Scribner's Sons, 1952).
[2] II Samuel 12.

question of what it is and the question of how it can be found, has to do, first of all, not with human institutions, but with the human being himself: that what one needs to ask first is not, "What is a just social order?", or "In what does true democracy consist?", but "What is man?"

—JOSEPH WOOD KRUTCH [3]

[3] *The Desert Year* (New York: William Sloane Associates; copyright Joseph Wood Krutch, 1952).

1: Theology and the "8:15"

One need not be a chamber—to be haunted—
One need not be a house—
The brain has corridors—surpassing material place—
Far safer, of a midnight meeting
External Ghost
Than its interior confronting—
That cooler host
Far safer, through an Abbey gallop,
The stones a'chase—
Than unarmed, one's own self encounter—
In lonesome place.
Ourself behind ourself, concealed
Should startle most. . . .

—"Estrangement"
by Emily Dickinson [1]

To ENCOUNTER oneself unarmed, in a lonesome place, is to experience the shock of recognition. It is to brush against the truth about oneself. Whether it be a David confronted by the prophet Nathan, or Socrates in full knowledge of his ignorance, or one of our contemporaries bored stiff with gadgets—self-recognition, as Emily Dickinson puts it mildly, "should startle most." The capacity for this shock of recognition is not only a reminder that our reflexes are still operational but also that we are summoned to this "lonesome place" for a look at ourselves. Apart from faith, unarmed, such encounters make up the repertory of our nightmares. And still, we are driven toward this solitary encounter. A man must know who he is, or else accept the spreading atrophy which proclaims his slow death in the midst of life.

I wonder if the prevailing fear of being alone is not grounded in our anxiety lest we reveal to ourselves, if to no other, what is stored in our hearts. Karl Menninger, the psychiatrist, writes: "There is everything to make us believe that man's chief fears are not the immensity of the universe but the *malignity* of his own aggressive instincts." [2] This assertion awakens an uneasiness within us. We remember that Jonah, who was possessed with anger, was chided in his sorrow for that *for which he had not labored*. Here perhaps, is another reason that we flee from the shock of recognition. We know only too well that we shall discover a heart devoid of treasured work—empty, save for the dust-laden years of wasted talents. To be a man is to know, even before we recognize it, that the meaning of life is constantly getting lost in the routine of the "8:15." We are a people who, even when we dash to catch the commuter train, are wondering if there is anyone or anything left inside worthy of the effort.

But man remains a curious paradox—a mixture of space and time, of finitude and infinitude. He is one whose identity gets submerged in a commuter culture on the move, and yet one destined for self-knowledge and eternity. It is just here that "Theology and the

'8:15' " meet. We propose to look at man through the
eyes of this contemporary—in relation to his own identity, the aspect of eternity and of the "8:15." The "8:15"
may be a commuter train or a bus or simply the reminder at the beginning of each day of our time-bound,
machine-dominated existence. W. H. Auden in his
Christmas play, "For the Time Being," uses this symbol
to recall that "let-down" mood which is apt to descend
upon us once the Christmas celebrations are over:

> . . . But, for the time being, here we all are,
> Back in the moderate Aristotelian city
> of darning and the Eight-Fifteen . . .
> There are bills to be paid, machines to keep
>   in repair . . . the Time Being to redeem
> From insignificance. . . .[3]

THE CLAIM OF THEOLOGY

Strictly speaking, theology is a highly specialized
discipline by which the assertions of faith are tested and
refined. As a science its task is not to proclaim the faith,
but to examine, relate, and verify it. Even so, most theologians today would hold that the task of theology
must be accomplished within the framework of faith.
The verbal assertions of belief can be neither fully
known nor understood by one who does not participate
in their related corporate life. This is not only true of
theology. There is a growing conviction in epistemology
that all knowledge involves some degree of participation on the part of the knower. Even the scientist, particularly in the area of human relations, must take
account of his own implicit relation to the known. It

follows, then, that in the case of theology (that is, knowledge of God) the traditional doctrines—such as those of creation and redemption, death and resurrection, guilt, repentance, and forgiveness—take on a more vital significance than the impersonality of a syllogism or a hypothesis. They become symbols of the meaning by which men live. It is in this sense of theology as *Weltanschau-ung* that we venture to speak of "Theology and the '8:15.'"

It is the claim of biblical theology that man's life in its whole dimension is seen only by making faith the presupposition of knowledge. This does not mean that faith is to be the censor of knowledge but rather its incentive. The Word of God becomes a mirror, as the epistle of James puts it, by which all men may see themselves. In that mirror the shock of recognition is administered with divine impartiality. Yet there is no mistaking the profoundly personal nature of this meeting. If to be a person is to struggle to discover oneself and a locus, a place, where one can *be* and *belong*, the mirror of God's word reveals both. Here supremely we are called by our name and that calling itself provides an ongoing relation where, as one of our folk songs has put it, we are "like a child at home." [4]

Further, our theology claims that reality itself is revealed as personal—that the earth, man and his history, even the mystery of our own rebirth are all the work of One who knows and searches us daily. Our history is God's history *in* and *through* us. History belongs to the realm of personal acts. Its prototypal action is set forth in the Nicene Creed: "*Who for us men and for our salvation came down from heaven, And was incarnate by the Holy Ghost of the Virgin Mary. . . ."*

The Church as the body of Christ holds itself to be nothing less than the pilgrimage home of the person. The distinctive character of the Church, however, is not a quantitative standard or a spatial location but an abiding and renewing relationship in which Christ himself is revealed. This means that if the Church is to be the Church it must proclaim the Word in such a way that the person is continually opened for new depths of truth. It cannot rely on "smooth sayings" and escapist religious talk.[5] Rather it must speak the truth in love. This means, more specifically, that the Church is alive only when it stands in judgment over against the person—remembering that judgment and grace are one in Christ. The Church and the person are held together by mutuality and tension. Every neglected, alienated person represents a visible judgment upon what we have made of the Church. Every person who approaches the full stature of manhood in Christ is a living witness to the power of God in the Church.

The claim of theology is that God overtakes and wounds us when we flee from the reckoning of this Presence. This is true whether our flight is into the Church or into the routine of the "8:15"! We know by faith also that God saves us, though all undeserving, by the miracle of grace. In both we are caught up in the shock of recognition.

OUR TIME AND THE ASPECT OF ETERNITY

The symbol "8:15" conveys something of our own attitude toward time. Unlike the monks who devised the clock as a means of keeping the hours for God's worship, we are encapsulated in time. It is the unyielding arbitor of our lives—in pain and in pleasure. Nietzsche said that man is a rope stretched across an abyss. For the world of the "8:15" that abyss is time.

But the meaning of time involves more than mere sequence—or an impersonal ordering of reality. It requires a transcendent agency which gathers up its meaning as does a melody in a song. It requires also one for whom time makes sense. In man that transcending quality is represented in his response *in kind* to the personal action of God in history. In a time of turmoil and change, Augustine tells us, he began to wonder who he was. That question and the self-recognition which ensued represented a significant reshaping of history for a thousand years to come. In Augustine the present moment was seen again under the aspect of eternity. The very insistence of his questioning opened the way for new vision. In like manner Dante conveyed to the medieval world through its own contemporaries the mode of life lived under the aspects of eternity—*sub specie aeternitatis*.

Time, then, is more than a perpetual counting. It is also the occasion of God's entry into and fulfillment of history. It is the event of Christ once and for all enacted on Calvary but *made present* on every new occasion. It is also our own creation anew out of nothing—in modern dress, so to speak.

Modern man lives under the aspect of the "8:15" and hopes thereby to avoid the disturbing questions aroused by the aspect of eternity. He shies away from the larger perspective by reducing time to small capsules or by devising means of "killing time." And all the while he finds himself bewildered by "time on his hands." He attempts to "domesticate" the Eternal, preferring a God who abandons the heavens and makes himself useful. Yet he is disconcerted by the shallowness of his own religion in times of crisis. He pays fabulous sums for a brief rental of power, speed, and mastery; and yet, like Pascal, he is frightened by the "eternal silence of these infinite spaces." The rope stretched across the abyss of time reaches its limits in moments of unavoidable stress—in guilt, in impotency, in the emptiness and meaninglessness of life which may be revealed in a look or a shrug of the shoulders. These are the moments of "infinite learning," as Kierkegaard put it. Under the shock of such revelation one may turn from flight into the recognition of himself as the object of God's love, notwithstanding his lack of merit. The opposite happens all too often: precisely in such stress and apart from faith one is confirmed in his avoidance of life. Many psychiatrists believe that neurosis is not merely a symptom but *a way of life*—something approaching a religion. It is a way of avoiding living by fracturing time into an infinite number of detours. It is to exist by putting off life!

OUR VOCATION IN GOD'S GRACE

Our "time" under the aspect of the "8:15" is leading us inexorably back to the crucial weakness of our implicit theology. We find ourselves staring unwittingly into the abyss of God's time. It is not only that in an age of space, men find themselves more often searching the heavens. Rather it is that God in revealing the limits of man's finitude also reveals the inadequacy of his *reason for being*. Our contemporary experience of space, infinity, and magnitude coincides with the empirical rediscovery of anxiety as the soil which nurtures both sin and guilt, freedom and creativity. No man comes to know himself *as human* apart from the pain of anxiety and the burden of responsibility. The story of the Fall in Eden is the story of every man: the cost of knowing is the burden of existence. Sin can no more be explained away than can the disquiet which batters the heart of every man. Listen:

> I am the man who has seen affliction under
>   the rod of his wrath. . . .
> Remember my affliction and my bitterness, the
>   wormwood and the gall! . . .
> But this I call to mind,
>   And therefore I have hope:
> The steadfast love of the Lord never ceases,
>   His mercies never come to an end;
> They are new every morning;
>   great is thy faithfulness.[6]

But this I call to mind! Here is a moment of profound recognition for all of us. To come to oneself is first of all a shock. But that shock and the bitterness which it entails may lead on to the profound recognition of ourselves as found in the steadfast love of God which never ceases, and yet, is new every morning. Here we are caught up in the movement from grace that is judgment, to grace that is gift.

Our vocation in God's Grace is one of response to the word of love which has called us into being. "I have called you by name, you are mine." [7] It may be that our first experience of that calling is our recognition that innocence is no longer ours, but guilt before God. To claim one's own responsibility in guilt is an act of freedom and a source of reconciliation which no man can accomplish apart from grace. It opens the way for forgiveness and the healing work of reparation. Another "first" response to our vocation is that we find ourselves as *participants* rather than as *spectators*. To know the love of God is to do his work: this conviction lies at the heart of biblical faith. We are placed on the stage of history; and our witness in action, such as it is, becomes the vehicle of God's action. As Charles Gore once put it, "What He does *for* us, He must ultimately do *in* us."

Perhaps the most dramatic change which comes from our vocation in God's grace is the movement from anxious possessiveness to a recognition of gift as the inner face of reality itself. This is the unguessed goodness of revelation. It is the mystery which is hidden from the oversophisticated, but revealed to the pure in heart. It was by this gift that the Samaritan *saw* the wounds of the broken man which the others ignored. Christ blessed the eyes which *see* and the ears which *hear:* To see and to hear is to love with a heart that knows the mysterious power of gift. G. K. Chesterton used to say that the Christian vision is to see and to hear and to know things *in their inherent mystery*. This seeing with surprise is at the heart of the gospel.

Luther has said that "the time of law (judgment) has an end; but the time of grace is eternal." This is the change which Christ has wrought in time. In faith we live *under* grace, not *under* law—and grace is inexhaustible. The bleak prospect of life dominated by the "8:15" is that it is lived under law rather than grace. It grinds away our life without replenishment. Theology and the "8:15" intersect each other in the moment of self-recognition. The shock of that experience may send us scampering for new hiding places; but that shock may also serve as the physician who leads us back to health. This happens when the time of grace incorporates and transcends the solitary moment of shock as the melody of a song embraces and extends the meaning of a single note.

• *Notes for Chapter 1*

1. Reprinted by permission of the publishers from *The Poems of Emily Dickinson,* Thomas H. Johnson, ed., Cambridge, Mass., The Belknap Press of Harvard University Press, copyright 1951, 1955, by The President and Fellows of Harvard College. Found in Vol. II, pp. 516-517.

For this reference I am indebted to Jean Merrill Balderson, "Emily Dickinson—Puritan, Neurotic, or Proto-Existentialist?" in *Bulletin,* Hartford Seminary Foundation, No. 27, May, 1959, pp. 23-41.

2. Karl Menninger, *Love Against Hate* (New York: Harcourt, Brace & Co., 1943), p. 190.

3. *The Collected Poetry of W. H. Auden* (New York: Random House, Inc., 1945), pp. 465-466.

4. A paraphrase of Psalm 23 from a Southern mountain hymn, tune arranged by Virgil Thomson. The last verse is particularly poignant: "There would I find a settled rest,/ While others go and come./ No more stranger or a guest/ But like a child at home."

5. Isaiah 30:9ff: ". . . speak to us smooth things, prophesy illusions. . . ." B. D. Napier, in *From Faith to Faith* (New York: Harper & Brothers, 1955), comments: "Give us a smooth covenant. Leave us with our illusion that all is well; that Yahweh is ours, and not we his."

6. Lamentations 3:1 and 19, and 21-23.

7. Isaiah 43:1.

2: The Person in a World of Technology

⋅§ "He who abides in me, and I in him, he it is that bears much fruit, for apart from me, you can do nothing." [1]

RECENTLY REINHOLD NIEBUHR suggested in a sermon at Union Theological Seminary that ours is probably the first civilization to be entirely dominated by its economy. Every part of our culture and every aspect of our personal life bears the imprint of our technology. The succeeding revolutions of steam, diesel, electric, and now atomic power have left their mark upon all that we do. Even home and church could not function adequately today, except as impressive witness to the wizardry of science. One Detroit industrialist is reported to have said (whether in pride or guilt I know not) that home is the place where the son waits for the return of the family automobile!

Does technology, then, mean the abolition of the person? What remains, what fragment, for the person to begin asking, "How much of me is me?" Simone Weil once said that it is easier for a non-Christian to become a Christian than for a "Christian" to become one. We get some clue for an understanding of what she meant

34

when we try to imagine ourselves living in a nontech-
nical world. It simply is impossible. The eyes that see
not and the ears that hear *not* have become adjusted to
a pervasive standard which hides the radical transformation of our world. The subtle shift from the scale of
the person to the scale of the mass eludes our attention.
We do not choose to become automata. We find that we
already are! In fact, prevailing standards have a way of
quietly possessing men's lives by becoming their own un-
witting expressions of expectations—and therefore
measures of esteem. The values of a technical world
have not been imposed upon us. We have embraced
them without resistance—not only in office, plant, and
laboratory, but also in home, school, and church. They
represent the anonymous authority which rules our
lives without our having consciously chosen them.

We can get some measure of our absorption in technological values by giving attention to these words of
Jesus: ". . . *Apart from me you can do nothing.*" Nothing? Is this word addressed to the same creature who
split the atom, tunneled the earth and its waters,
bridged its valleys, and scaled its heights? No—surely
the poet is nearer the truth when he exults in the feats
of this creature called man who by his own ingenuity
and audacity has

> . . . slipped the surly bonds of earth . . .
> Put out my hand and touched the face of God.[2]

Is this nothing?

Ronald Knox in his translation of our text renders it
as follows: ". . . *If a man lives on in me, and I in him,
then he will yield abundant fruit; separated from me*

you have no power to do anything." These words stir faint echoes in our minds of that curious *helplessness* which we so often feel in the presence of great mechanical power. A push-button world does not save our marriages—nor our relation to our children. Indeed, it only punctuates our impotence as well as the hazards of existence itself in a world where "summit talks" can end so precipitously. The Greek word for *nothing* here emphasizes absolute negation—not a mere lack of potential. Apart from God in Christ all that man can do is as nothing. The nearest analogy which comes to my mind is the description of that utter desolation in the book of Isaiah when the prophet is told how long he must proclaim God's word to a people who have eyes but see not and ears but hear not: "Until cities lie waste without inhabitant, And houses without men, And the land is utterly desolate. . . ." [3] The "nothingness" of our world lies hidden behind the chrome surface and mechanical efficiency of our technology. It is a concealed malignancy which feeds upon our sense of helplessness and futility. Mechanical advance has steadily removed the burdens we have used to justify what we are. No wonder automation is such a menace; it not only threatens to render the worker obsolete, but it also promises to expose the emptiness of our life apart from task orientation. Meanwhile we rush frantically through life hoping to delay this exposure or at least find some relevance for ourselves in its direction. Our problem is no longer one of subsistence, but of finding a reason for existence.

A FALSE DILEMMA

There is a false dilemma which is common to modern man and is evident in his attitude toward techniques. Either he is completely taken over by and identified with machine values or he tends to despise or to reject them while ignoring his dependence upon them. The words "techniques" and "manipulation" have acquired the significance of value. It is easily forgotten that the machine is a neutral instrument. It has not subverted us, but our inordinate desire for and use of its power has debased it. Indeed, in terms of function the machine has greatly extended the power of the individual *for* communication and communion. Techniques make civilization possible. Their true function, like any deliberate habit, is to free the person to be himself. They are the expected fruits of a liberal, or liberating, society where grievous burdens are lifted from man's back and he is free to pursue the peculiar talents which men possess. Instead, our false dilemma about this power—and its limits—tends to reinforce the persistent idea that man is helpless beside such strength and, even worse, that he is not responsible.

But such an attitude strikes at the very root of our freedom in Christ. We forget that God in Christ has not left us helpless before the principalities and powers of this world. To be sure, our transcendent freedom in Christ does not automatically resolve our problem with technical power; but, certainly, it alters the character of our dependency. If it is true, as Paul writes, that "there is no authority except from God," [4] then the genuine source of our authority is clear, even if our use of power is delinquent. "It is he who sits above the circle of the earth," Deutero-Isaiah reminded his generation. The uniqueness of man lies just here: that by faith and trust in Him who sits above the circle of the earth he is delivered from the bondage of encircling technology. Freedom is the only proper mode of response to God—the source of all authority. It should be doubly clear to us, then, that the deeper tragedy of a generation ensnared by its own techniques and characterized by its "other-directedness" is the prevailing image that man is nothing but a passive recipient of forces.

MAN IS MAN-BEFORE-GOD

We are confused about the person in a world of technology because we have forgotten who man is. The biblical view of man rests upon these three fundamental affirmations which are laid down in Genesis:

• Creation is the work of God's hands.

• Man is made in the image and likeness of God as one intended to share in creative work.

• Man is not made for himself alone but for relationship. Hence man's identity (that is, his true power of being) is to be found in the depths of love and response.

If this is accepted as the portrait of man *before God,* its opposite, namely, *man apart from God,* could hardly have been put more poignantly than in Paul's words: "And if I have prophetic powers, and understand all mysteries and all knowledge and if I have all faith, so as to remove mountains, but have not love, I am nothing." [5]

I wonder if the whole problem of man in a world of technology does not go back to a mistaken notion which conceives the purpose of scientific knowledge within the narrow bounds of understanding, prediction, and control. Is it not possible that modern technology has let the depth of "understanding" atrophy while primarily concerned with "prediction" and "control"? One has only to raise the question, "To what purpose?" and it is evident that prediction and control are not enough. To be sure, the great scientists like Henri Poincaré insist that the scientist does not study nature because it is useful but because "he delights in it, and he delights in it because it is beautiful." Even so, beyond delight, we ask, is it possible to *know* anything unless we are willing to love it? Even nature does not yield her secrets at second hand. We are slowly learning that all knowledge is participative—that one is profoundly related to all that he knows. Sin and its consequent alienation, therefore, represent the desire to manipulate rather than to love, to use rather than to relate.

Is not this one deep significance of the myth of the fall? What Adam sought was more than food—more than the enjoyment of God's good earth. He was enticed by the whispered promise of rivalry with God as a means of sustaining himself in proud isolation. Here is the origin of guilt as well as creativity. Guilt is the stain left behind when freedom is squandered on anything less than genuine relation; creativity is a priceless gem always purchased in the knowledge of the irreducible hazard of freedom. It is not without significance that in our day the sense of guilt is most pronounced precisely where the power of technology is most multiplied—among our nuclear physicists. The dark abyss of freedom is a terrifying reality for those who have discovered that the multiplication of power is still in the hands of one who is free to choose life or death.

OUR LABOR OUR PRAYER

Yet according to the biblical admonition in Genesis such a one is to have dominion over earth. As James Moffatt puts it, he is to "master" the earth. What is it to master the earth? In the Hebrew language there is a deep association between mastery and fatherhood. The farmer is master of his land and its crops not as an absentee lord but as a father who knows and nurtures his children. Again, mastery in this sense of kinship as well as differentiation is a valid description of the child's growing awareness of his own relation to the world. Perhaps there is a clue to the meaning of this dimension of mastery in the child's discovery of shape and tactility. Observers tell us that at first the child is unable to grasp an object because the thumb and fingers are not in juxtaposition to each other. Gradually, however, the child acquires this grasping ability and there comes a time when he "recognizes" an object as something distinct from himself and yet related to him as a shape to which his thumb and fingers conform. Is this acquisition of tactility the origin of man's ability to make tools—and to employ sacrament? Surely mastery, in the sense that we are using the word, represents another analogy for the image of God in man. Man's dominion is to be exercised in such a way that every instrument reflects the sacramental relation between creator and creation.

Our vocation as persons requires the uniting of meaning and work in a manner which many find increasingly difficult in this world of technology. We dare not forget the extent to which the machine has isolated work from the rest of life. Mass production and technical specialization make it difficult in the extreme to unite work and meaning. Yet this is our task. Perhaps we need to look for more realistic ways of combining work and play in worship. That each is a separate compartment now is some indication of our scattered lives. Some lines from G. K. Chesterton remind us that

> When folk forget the dance and song,
> Women wash useless pots the whole day long.

Our vocation as persons is to make our labor our prayer—*laborare est orare.* The mode of our work is incarnational—always bearing in our bodies the spirit of Christ, always beholding his image in those whom we meet. Dorothy Day, whose spirit is the heart of the *Catholic Worker* movement, tells of a statue of St. Joseph in front of their Bowery house of hospitality. Men tip their hats as they pass and frequently Italian women curtsy. "One evening," Dorothy Day writes, "there was a man lying on the street pavement close up against our house, his knees up to his chest, his head on his arm. He was asleep. An Italian woman who could not speak English very well seized my arm as I came up. I could scarcely understand her, but she kept pointing to the man saying in turn, 'Jesus Christ . . . my son, my heart is broken.'" "He wasn't really her son," Dorothy Day explained, "but she knew what she was talking about. He was Jesus Christ, shocking as it may seem, drunk as he was."

And truth is conveyed in this earthen vessel. Apart from Christ, all our working is nothing. Abiding in him, we bear much fruit; for in every person who addresses us and claims our deep response there speaks also the voice of one who is Lord of our life and fashioner of all that we do.

• *Notes for Chapter 2*

1. John 15:5b.
2. From "High Flight," by John G. Magee, Jr., 19-year-old American pilot killed in December, 1941, in service with the Royal Canadian Air Force.
3. Isaiah 6:11.
4. Romans 13:1.
5. I Corinthians 13:2.

3: Who Cares in a World of Caretakers?

> ❧ By lavish and progressive measures
> Our neighbor's wants are all relieved;
> We are not called to share his pleasures
> And in his grief we are not grieved.[1]

IT IS THE CONTENTION of the existentialist writer, Albert Camus, that the underlying motif of contemporary society is one of "dodging judgment." Our whole way of life is a grand *tour de force;* its main purpose is to avoid responsibility and to maintain at least the appearance of innocence. The frantic scramble for money has for its goal the protection it affords. In the novel, *The Fall,* the narrator explains to his confidant: "Wealth, *cher ami,* is not quite acquittal, but reprieve, and that's always worth taking."[2]

More light is shed on this propensity of modern man for dodging judgment when we consider what has happened to the human capacity for caring. To care is to expose oneself to some degree of commitment, and commitment always involves judgment. On the face of it our welfare states in contemporary history are built upon the foundation of human caring. The "pursuit of happiness" and the "general welfare" mentioned in our own country's founding articles have become incentives for broad humanitarian programs. The specter of unemployment, the grievous burden of poverty and overwork and the shadow of an embarrassed old age which have been more or less removed by these programs are gains with which only a misanthropist could find reason to quarrel.

But along with the gains of the welfare state there is a disturbing atrophy of the human spirit. What happens when the individual gives over to the state his responsibility for caring? The motive for caring becomes abstracted and generalized like so many other activities in modern technical society. The heart of care tends to be replaced by a bureaucratic process of manipulating people into an attitude of well-being. That this deterioration of caring does not always happen is a tribute to the humanity of many teachers, doctors, social workers, and clinicians. Apart from their heroic effort the institutionalization of human caring favors the development of a vast army of caretakers whose vision is colored by an impersonal norm and who increasingly distrust personal deviations. Here is the incipient danger of every welfare state: its dependence upon technology may destroy the very humanity to which it is dedicated. There is genuine pathos as well as satire in Albert Camus' portrait of "The Stranger" who had been nurtured in such a climate and who, when chided about his callousness at his mother's funeral, reports, "I answered that of recent years, I'd rather lost the habit of noting my feelings, and hardly know what to answer."

Who cares in a world of caretakers? I suspect that all

of us want deeply to love and to be loved, but the impersonality of contemporary life provides a ready means of escape from the pain and responsibility of caring. Perhaps even deeper, we have experienced the shock of recognizing that not one of us is able to maintain a loving relationship out of our own resources. Our loud protestations of good intention often hide our inability to love. It becomes brutally evident that Christ's words are true: *Apart from Me you can do nothing.* Apart from faith man remains an isolate. He is propelled from outside. Where he touches the lives of others, in marriage, in work, even in death, he is alone and pathetically impotent. In order to survive in such a world, one must learn not to care. Perhaps you have seen Abner Dean's cartoon of a solitary individual riding high on a one-wheel cycle while hordes of other solitary individuals mill about below. The legend proclaims: "The trick is in not caring!"

THE CARETAKER ATTITUDE

Actually the last century has witnessed a passionate search on the part of man to find genuine community. The age-old longing in man's soul for a city whose builder and founder is God has become in our time the search for the ideal political state. One need not look too closely in order to discover the residual motif which remains in the drive for a kind of religious community and liturgy in the prevailing political philosophies of today. In the Communist states with their zeal, their conviction that progress is on their side, their orthodoxy, holy persons, and shrines, the quasi-religious tone is

obvious. What may not be obvious is the fact that
liberal capitalism is also buttressed by certain popular
assumptions which carry the weight of religion. But
since these assumptions are hardly ever critically ex-
amined in our secularized culture, we are blind to their
propensity to outrage others. Consider the prevailing
attitude that our technical progress is proof of our virtue
and industriousness. The underlying assumption which
tends to equate godliness and mass production often
issues in ill-mannered and self-righteous behavior toward those who would like to use our machines to help
feed their hungry, but who cannot stomach our arro-
gance.

The truth is that where the caretaker attitude pre-
vails, man is reduced to a cipher. His needs are sup-
plied, but human response is neither given nor evoked.
In such a climate it appears that the food or goods
which one is able to provide by the wizardry of his technology becomes a kind of magic which is substituted
for the human concern which might have been given.
The personhood of both the dispenser and the recipient
is robbed by such an attitude. Indeed, the responsible
person is prevented from ever reaching maturity. The
person becomes a commodity, and his eternal soul acquires a price tag. That this happens in Christendom,
and has been happening for some time, was vividly
demonstrated by Kierkegaard, who wrote,

> In Christendom the immediate man, too, is a Christian;
> he goes to church every Sunday; hears and understands
> the Parson; Yea, they understand one another; he dies;
> the Parson introduced him into eternity for the price of

ten dollars—but a self he was not, and a self he did not become.[3]

The caretaker attitude must be understood in terms of the basic model of man and of reality which stands behind it. Since Descartes, whose formula, "I think, therefore I am" left an impassable gulf between the thinking mind and man's being, modern man has sought to find an explanation for his behavior which is centered in the organism rather than in the will or intention. Today man's thinking about himself and his society is dominated by one of several models, all of which represent abstractions from the whole being. Let us explore briefly three of these:

First, there is the psychological model. In psychoanalysis the prevailing view understands man's behavior in terms of *libido*. Sexual fulfillment in its widest connotation provides an empirical basis for knowledge of the affective drives. Other psychological views may emphasize the avoidance of anxiety or the repetition of learned patterns, but many models reflect a common assumption that behavior is simply a function of forces beyond human intention. Man is more the recipient of action than its initiator. The concept of will is replaced by such causal categories as "reflex," "cathexis," and "dynamism." It is difficult to see how in terms of such a model, the act of love can be an act of the person at all. It is tension reduction. Love in any larger or more affiliative sense is but a chimera, a delusion.

Second, there is the socio-political model which seeks to explain man's behavior in terms of the drive for power. We may remember that for Nietzsche all social behavior is either direct or disguised power seeking. Even gratitude, he held, is nothing more than "a good revenge" which one takes in order to re-establish his own potency in social relationships. It would be easy to dismiss this view as alien if we let ourselves forget how closely it approximates the rationale of classical Western capitalism. Thomas Hobbes, it may be remembered, proclaimed self-interest and power to be the irreducible basis of social relations. Likewise it was Adam Smith and his interpreters who, in the words of Karl Marx, "left no other nexus between man and man than naked self-interest, than callous 'cash payment.'" It is interesting to note that the German Christian economist Adam Müller [4] (1779-1829) deplored the breach between capitalists and laborers which resulted from the removal of the tools from the ownership of those who worked with them. He predicted the atomization of human personality in a technological society where division and mechanization of labor prevailed.

Third, the Marxian model for man reflects its revolt against the devaluation of man as mere labor by proclaiming that man's behavior always betrays and is determined by its economic motive. Marx declared, "The proletarians have nothing to lose but their chains. They have a world to win. Working-men of all countries unite!" I wonder if we can imagine something of the appeal of this slogan to the hopeless people of the world? If their predominant image of American economic policy is gained from "The Ugly Americans" (as our caretaker representatives have been called), is it any wonder that they find excitement and hope in the Marxist dream? That most of the abuses in earlier capi-

talism have been corrected appears to be uncommu-
nicated in our massive propaganda exchanges. Even so
the Marxian illusion that the removal of individual
wealth will put an end to the power struggle and
duplicity among men is justly exposed and satirized in
George Orwell's "Animal Farm." Though it is true, we
are reminded, that all men are equal, some men are
more equal than others!

MAN: WHAT A PIECE OF WORK

The truth is that no abstraction is adequate for an
understanding of man in his totality. But it is equally
true that there is an element of authenticity in each of
these prospects if we accept their necessary reduction
of man. Further, in view of the fact that these models
in one form or another are the prevailing ones in our
social and intellectual climate, it seems clear that here
we have the major factor in the origin and propagation
of the caretaker attitude. If contemporary man is "enchanted by secularized thinking" as Hendrik Kraemer
has put it, his disenchantment must begin with an unmasking of his favorite models along with a serious
challenge to the adequacy of the knowledge which they
yield.

The biblical picture of man, on the other hand, includes the ambiguities which emotional distortion,
power seeking, and motives of economic gain represent,
but it contains more. As the actual history of a covenant
people who continually betray their trust, turn back to
slavery, but never quite lose the saving remnant, the
biblical story is one of *intentions* rather than *motives,*

of *acts* rather than *behavior*. Its subject matter is persons and their actions, and, as John Macmurray has written, "In a strict sense of the term only a person can 'act' or in the proper sense 'do' anything." [5]

"What a piece of work is a man!" Shakespeare is impressed with the sublime in man. Even in demoralization and defeat his men and women are sublime. Where is this vision of man in our day? Is it just possible that in our snickering at man's foibles we have lost our capacity to see him whole? Interestingly enough it was Freud's fascination with classic figures in history which kept him from a radical and final reduction of man to the level of a mechanical object. In this, as in many other areas, Freud was ambiguous. He was drawn to and deeply moved by the figure of Moses; yet he would have rejected the faith of Moses as illusory. In one of his papers he tells of his frequent visits to Michelangelo's Moses in the Church of San Pietro in Vincoli in Rome. "Sometimes," he wrote, "I have crept cautiously out of the half-gloom of the interior as though I myself belonged to the mob upon whom his eye is turned—the mob which can hold fast no conviction, which has neither faith nor patience and which rejoices when it has regained its illusory idols." [6]

We are coming more and more to the conviction that every model of man which depends upon an abstraction is not only inadequate; it may also be injurious. The psychological abstractions, for instance, are helpful in viewing behavior from this selected perspective. But most therapists would surely agree that the process of psychotherapy includes many factors not accounted for in psychological theory. The wise therapist, like the

mature grandmother of another era, learns the art of
being helpful, which goes beyond mere theory. Psychological models become injurious when they are in-
dulged as generalizations for human behavior. They
tend to leave the impression that man is merely the
passive recipient of forces—never an initiator of action.
Thus, the nerve of responsibility—indeed of human caring itself—is severed.

The caretaker world would have us believe that man
is the product of forces beyond himself. It is not necessary to deny the importance of these forces in shaping
the person, when we assert, even so, "in action how
like an angel!" The person is neither known nor defined
in his totality by reference to his social group or clinical
record. If any human being is to be known or defined,
it must be in the arena of action. Man is man only when
he takes action. Neither he nor his moral values can
be reduced to abstractions. The essence of "moralism"
is just such abstractionism. To be human is to be mor-
ally responsible; and such responsibility does not consist of a state of mind or of a set of beliefs but of a mode
of action. The caretaker world sacrifices the person to
an absurd norm and this is the source of its pernicious
influence. While he was a prisoner in Russia after the
Second World War, Helmut Gollwitzer,[7] a former German chaplain, witnessed the destruction of a bumper
crop of sugar beets while he and his fellow prisoners
as well as the natives were near starvation. This was
done because a minor official had misjudged the
projected yield. Here is a foretaste of a world in which
accurate predictions are likely to be more important
than persons.

CARING: HUMAN AND DIVINE

Who cares in a world of caretakers? In order to answer the question we must return to our first statement: As long as man is bent on dodging judgment, as long as he prefers to barter his soul for the satiation of captivity, human caring, as well as human being, is extinct. We remember that the Grand Inquisitor in Dostoyevsky's novel *The Brothers Karamazov* declared in opposition to the freedom of Christ that one who would rule men must hold their conscience and their bread in his hands. The caretaker would dispense bread for selected needs and offers explanations for questions which arise from man's conscience.

But, strangely enough, humanity does not always prefer the tinseled comforts of captivity. A man may forget who he is but he cannot forever deny what he is: namely, one made in the image and likeness of God. There come moments of decision, issues which cannot be evaded; and one remembers, as he is faced by the inescapable alternative of God: "Who is on my side? Who?" [8] Edward Steichen in his remarkable collection of photographs, "The Family of Man," places that text under the chiseled features of a black man: "Who is on my side? Who?"

We come to ourselves in the shock of recognizing that we are, after all, addressed from beyond ourselves. We are, in fact, judged. We are expected to respond and to claim our own manhood. Some years ago Justice Cardozo ruled in favor of a petitioner who had gone to the rescue of another and had himself been accidentally injured. The Justice wrote: "Danger invites rescue. The

cry of distress is the summons to relief." The deepest
motive in man is to care lovingly and, in turn, to be
cared for. To ignore the cry of distress which is a
summons to relief is disobedience to one's own humanity. It is failure to hear, or to love, or to give attention.

Hence, to claim one's own humanity is to recognize
that the lovelessness of the world is rooted in the lovelessness of one's own heart. The absence of love will not
be cured by programs or law, although the law may
provide the minimum structure in which justice is
possible. The cure of our lovelessness is mediated
through the little death we are willing to die in claiming
our own sin. It is replenished in the continual bearing
in our bodies of the death of Christ as we learn to
care again. This, simply, is the fulfillment of our bap-
tismal vow.

Christian care is not some prize for spiritual discipline. It is not a technique nor a device. It is rather
the quickening of our hearts as we participate in the
supreme care of Jesus Christ. No man is able to care
unless he is *a new man in* Christ. And no man is *new*
except in the wake of judgment and forgiveness. William Blake realized this when he wrote:

> I forgive you
> You forgive me
> This is the bread
> This is the blood of eternity.

Our caring as Christians is a visible renewal of that
steadfast love of God which is also mysteriously new
every morning. To live by that love is to care for the

finishing of God's work. In a world of caretakers we need the daily reminder of Meister Eckhart's words:

> God lies in wait for us with nothing
> So much as Love. . . . Love is like a
> fisherman's hook. . . . That we may
> All be so caught and set free,
> May he help us, who is love itself.[9]

• *Notes for Chapter 3*

1. Dorothy Sayers, "The Vigil of the Enlightenment," *Punch*, Nov., 1953. By permission of David Higham Associates, Ltd.

2. Albert Camus, *The Fall* (New York: Alfred A. Knopf, Inc., 1957), p. 82.

3. Sören Kierkegaard, *Sickness unto Death*, W. Lowrie, trans. (Princeton, N.J.: Princeton University Press, 1941), p. 6.

4. See George Soule, *Ideas of the Great Economists* (New York: Mentor Books, 1952).

5. John Macmurray, *The Self as Agent* (New York: Harper & Brothers, 1937), pp. 88-89.

6. Sigmund Freud, *Collected Papers* (London: Hogarth Press, Ltd.) Vol. IV, pp. 259-260.

7. See Helmut Gollwitzer, *Unwilling Journey* (Philadelphia: Muhlenberg Press, 1953).

8. II Kings 9:32.

9. Sermon No. 4, *Meister Eckhardt*, Raymond B. Blakney, trans. (New York: Harper & Brothers, 1941), Harper Torch Book, pp. 123-124.

4: The End of Man?

New York City had just completed one of its recurrent civil defense exercises. With astonishing abruptness its multifarious activities had come to a halt. The newspapers published pictures of the busiest intersection in the world completely emptied of people. The familiar scene in the heart of the city gave the impression of a ghost town—bereft and strangely muted in midday.

The empty city beholding itself on the verge of destruction calls to mind another scene when Christ stood looking down on Jerusalem from the hills above. That great city was also uneasy about its peace. It had stoned its prophets, and soon its narrow streets would echo the sound of the mob: "Crucify him, crucify him!" The climax of this scene is a portrayal of the subsequent disaster of Jerusalem. Christ is speaking, as translated by Ronald Knox: "Behold your house is left to you, a house uninhabited."

In both incidents the great city is seen by anticipation as "a house uninhabited." Is this recurring image of man's total annihilation, as in the story of Noah and the flood, a reminder of our precarious tenancy of the earth? Is the evacuation of our cities a way of anticipating the end of man? In Noah's time, it is the Lord who is portrayed as One grieved by his own Creation and resolving to "blot out man . . . from the face of the ground." [1] In our case the vacant streets of the world's most populated city suggests something of our already lost humanity—of the disappearance of man.

The symbol of a world uninhabited because it is filled with Kafka-like, anonymous creatures is not unfamiliar to this age. Indeed, it is a familiar theme in our plays and novels. In Samuel Beckett's play, "Endgame," one of the characters reflects, "I say to myself that the earth is extinguished, though I never saw it lit." [2]

A darkened world is another way of expressing the loss of communal meaning by a people who have never really known what it means to be themselves. To have lived without such self-discovery is to serve out one's days under the dark shadow of the end of man.

OUR LOST HUMANITY

When man lives under the shadow of his own lost humanity, his daily life slips through his hands like watery sand sucked under by a strong current. He comes from his feverish effort to grasp life, emptyhanded. His countenance is familiar. Most of us know this strange defeat. Having gained a world of creature comfort, we have lost or misplaced the creature himself, that is, man. We like to think that the crushing out of the individual is the work of the state or the encroachment of technology. We shudder in the grip of a novel like George Orwell's *1984*. But we forget that the choice is our own. We forget that man who was intended for dialogue with his Creator was also endowed with freedom and the capacity for decision. If man is to disappear, then, it will be the logical outcome of his own acts—the ineluctable result of the kind of world which he has chosen.

Even so, we make a practice of hiding or ignoring our own responsibility. Only when the result of our decisions is immediate and inescapable are we likely to take notice. Kierkegaard once said that the loss of the real self passes unnoticed! If one loses an arm or a leg, the loss is immediately and painfully noticed. But the self slips away without incident—its only reminder is a vague sense of vacuity which always seems to require something more than we can attain.

Let me suggest three habitual modes of thinking where this loss of humanity is revealed but still unrecognized by us:

First, we are a people who talk a great deal about "being ourselves," but we are never satisfied with the selves we are. There is a curious paradox here of self-idolatry which is at the same time self-rejection. Like the classic figure of Faust, modern man is always on the look-out for a deal whereby he may sell his soul (which he despises) for some magic power (which becomes his idol). We are forever looking for ways to exchange the selves we think we are for the streamlined version we think we ought to be. Thomas Wolfe described this habit as being characteristic of the great colony of lost Americans "who feel that everything is going to be all right with them if they can only take a trip, or learn a rule, or meet a person. . . ." Even a new breakfast cereal is credited with remarkable rejuvenating power!

This frantic seeking after a new model of ourselves plays into the hands of manipulators of every variety. It is a temptation to popular religion in which the cost of profound searching required of the new man in Christ is reduced to cheap grace. Verbal formulae, extravagant promises (which are cruel in their naïveté) grafted upon utter self-contempt are a poisonous concoction whether in religion or in politics. In this sense Eric Hoffer is quite justified when he writes: "Faith in a holy cause is to a considerable extent a substitute for the lost faith in ourselves." [3]

Second, we are a people who take pride in our freedom of choice but are harried—and even frightened—by any decision. Richard Eberhart has put it succinctly:

> It is borne in upon me that pain
> Is essential. The bones refuse to act.
> Recalcitrancy is life's fine flower.
> The human being is a lonely creature.[4]

There are those who claim that modern history can be understood only in terms of its dominant motif: namely, man's drive to escape from freedom. The tragedy of man, they say, is that as human and free, he cannot escape responsibility for himself. Yet his life is one long search for authorities who are willing to take over and manage his destiny. In a world of masses where knowledge of the whole is lost in diversified production, the loneliness of the person is accentuated. Here is a government employee who is conscientious in his work but is increasingly aware of the growing complications of policy questions. A decision which appears to be right today may tomorrow become the target of political investigation and attack. What is he to do? Without the courage and integrity of a transcending purpose he forfeits his freedom. He "plays safe." Again there is the housewife who is so anxious to prove her "enlightened attitude" that she raises her child by the latest pseudo-psychological bulletins—which change with the weather. And all the while both mother and child suffer from that loss of a real relationship rooted in the deep affinities of love which might have given both the courage to be themselves.

Third, our lost humanity is evident in what we call the "drivenness" of our lives. We like to picture ourselves as acting not from our own will or intention but from the diverse expectations of others. We are the passive ones whose destiny is not "to do or to die" but, apparently, to enjoy being questioned by our pollsters, as we are pushed or pulled by every power but our own. Our favorite pastime seems to be that of either writing or reading sociological surveys of our own plight. We weep for ourselves who are the victims of "other direction"; we see ourselves in the image of the "organization man," or caught in the rut of the "status seekers" or submerged in "suburban captivity." We weep—but our tears are momentary. We are not moved with a passion for the recovery of our humanity.

There is an apocryphal story of a harried clergyman who developed the mysterious habit of disappearing each day just after noon. In time this peculiarity was noticed by his parishioners who, being discreet, asked the Bishop to investigate. Subsequently the Bishop in his car followed the man from his church through the winding streets to that section where the railroad passed through town. The parson stopped and waited. So did the Bishop. Presently the daily streamliner roared past. After a few moments the minister was about to leave when he was hailed by the Bishop and asked to explain. With some embarrassment the minister replied, "Bishop, that train is the only damn thing in my parish which runs without my pushing it. I cannot resist the temptation to come here and admire it!" In a world where most things are either pushed or pulled the sight of a streamliner yields its own therapy!

THE WRATH THAT IS GRACE

Paul also recognized that man is caught in the mesh of his own conflicting expectations. The law written in the heart of every man will not acquiesce in the forfeiter of one's humanity. Conscience is a reminder that we are the major architects of our own betrayal. Frequently what we refer to as the drivenness of our lives is called simply "the wrath of God" in the Bible. And on first shock that wrath has the same effect as the contemporary recognition "that the earth is extinguished." In one of our most familiar psalms we read, "For when Thou art angry all our days are gone . . . like a sigh!" [5]

The Bible is full of instances where man, caught in what he believed to be the wrath of God, comes to the amazing realization that the very pain of this relationship means that one is still in the presence and care of God. Wrath is our perception of God's response to our protest, "Let me alone." Grace is the fact that God never leaves us alone. Job finally came to this astonishing realization when in the midst of his complaining he opened his eyes to exclaim:

> And Thou wilt fasten upon such!
> Thou wilt bring him to justice,
> His life all rotting in decay
> Like a moth-eaten robe! [6]

The grace of God that appears as wrath recalls the responsibility of man's humanity. Here one is called upon—addressed in person. The response could be to claim one's freedom through faith and trust in God. It may be flight. In either case the decision belongs to man. Perhaps you recall the words of the Grand Inquisitor in Dostoyevsky's novel. "For fifteen centuries," he said to Christ defiantly, "we have been wrestling with *Thy* freedom, but now it is ended and over for good. . . . Men desire to give up their freedom. . . ."

Yes, but then there is the fact of Christ. In him God does not take our first word as our last word. In Christ such a one is reminded that he was intended for freedom and fashioned for beatitude. In Christ God does not let us alone—even from the cross!

THE END WHICH IS THE BEGINNING

We began with the recurring image of man's disappearance from the earth. In God's grace the end of man becomes a new beginning. Immediately after the account of God's resolve to "blot out man . . . from the face of the ground" there follows the statement, "But Noah found favor in the eyes of the Lord." [7]

But Noah! But Christ! Here is the end of man which is also his new beginning. Here, like the prodigal son, we are found beyond our lost humanity in the unfailing love of the Father which is new every morning. But there is still one condition: Grace requires response. Love is no less love if rejected; but he who rejects love leaves himself to self-destruction. In order to recover ourselves, to come to ourselves, it is required that we claim our part in that dialogue with the eternal Father which involves both our freedom and our responsibility.

Here is a parable that may point up the final dilemma of man's freedom and humanity. Long ago before Eden, before man was given dominion over the earth, God decided to give all animals, including man, the gift of freedom. There was one provision: it was to be a period of testing; if after a time they had learned its secret, they were to be relieved of its torture. In due time the animals gathered before the Lord to report.

The jaguar spoke for the beasts of the forests: "When first I knew the gift of freedom," he said, "I looked out over the earth with all its wealth and possessions, and I wanted these things for myself. But after a while I remembered that the Lord of the earth had given me life and food. "So," he concluded, "I resolved to use my freedom to tell the beasts of the forests of my discovery, that 'all things come of Thee, O Lord.'" "Thou hast learned the secret of freedom," God said. "Return to the forest."

Then the eagle reported for the fowls of the heavens: "I knew freedom," he said, "as I soared high above the earth. All created things looked up to me and I thought how wonderful it would be to make them worship and

glorify me. But then it came to me," the eagle continued, "that my every flight must come to an end—that
Thou alone remainest. Then I decided to use my freedom to scream this message to the skies: "O worship
the Lord in the beauty of holiness, let the whole earth
stand in awe of him." "Thou too hast learned the secret
of freedom," the Lord declared. "Return to the skies."

The whale was the spokesman for the dwellers of the
sea. "With freedom," he declared, "I knew my power
and my strength. I considered how exhilarating it would
be to plough the ocean, sending all things in terror before me. But then I reflected that I am appointed to
live and that I am appointed to die. Thou rulest all
things. After that I went about reminding my fellow
creatures that "they who wait upon the Lord shall renew their strength." The whale was sent back to his
dwelling place.

It was man's turn to speak. "This freedom is a burdensome thing," he complained. "With it I have been
so taken up with possessions, so anxious to maintain
my place among the other creatures and so frightened
about the possibility of losing it, I have not had time to
learn its secret." "You shall have time," the Lord replied. So until this day man struggles to learn the secret
of freedom—both dreading its loss and in rare moments
of trust offering it again to God in praise and thanksgiving.

• *Notes for Chapter 4*

1. Genesis 6:7.

2. Samuel Beckett, "Endgame" (New York: Grove Press, Evergreen Books, 1958).

3. Eric Hoffer, *The True Believer* (New York: Mentor Books, 1958), p. 22.

4. Richard Eberhart, "The Human Being Is a Lonely Creature," in *New Poems,* Rolfe Humphries, ed. (New York: Ballantine Books, Inc. 1933).

5. Psalm 90:9, The Book of Common Prayer (BCP).

6. Job 14:3 (Moffatt).

7. Genesis 6:8.

PART TWO

The Trinity and the Roots of Our Identity

Then is all the whole Trinity intimate to us in every creature: and hence is the original form and perfection of that
holy city whereof the angels are inhabitants.

Augustine
in *The City of God*

If thou be far from thine own self, how canst thou draw near
to God?

Augustine
in *Joan. Evang.* XXIII

O God who art ever the same, let me know myself, let me
know Thee.

Augustine
in *Soliloquia*, II,i,1

5: We Are Persons After the Mode of Heaven

Blessed be the God and Father of our Lord Jesus Christ! By his great mercy we have been born anew to a living hope through the resurrection of Jesus Christ from the dead, and to an inheritance which is imperishable, undefiled, and unfading, kept in heaven for you. . . .[1]

SOME TIME AGO Robert Frost, the poet, was interviewed in connection with a forthcoming book of poetry. The author explained that his theme was that "the only *event* in all history is science plunging deeper into matter . . . but not without fear that the spirit shall be lost." A fragment from one of the poems runs like this:

> But God's own descent
> Into flesh was meant
> As a demonstration
> That the supreme merit
> Lay in risking spirit
> In substantiation.[2]

To risk spirit in substantiation, to invest eternity in existence—this is essentially what is meant by the New Testament affirmation: "And the Word became flesh!"

Now that event, coupled with the resurrection event, means that God has not only invested his love in the substantiality of persons, but also that his faithfulness continues with them until, as Peter says, we are "born anew to a living hope . . . imperishable, undefiled, and unfading, kept in heaven. . . ."

As persons we know almost too much about the opposite process, that is, death in the midst of life. Our days are like shadows which are forever casting the reflection of wasted years before us—of promises unkept and of bright hopes tarnished by time. We are bewildered by the strangeness of relationships which have not matured and of a pedestrian existence where our joys and pains are recorded in uneventful anonymity. Even more in our contemporary world of technology where machines are more important than persons and manipulation becomes a characteristic mode of existence, the identity of the person is apt to fall before the passion of fashioning all men after the wheel!

This is the same human predicament which is the occasion of God's risking himself—eternally and lovingly—for humanity. As Jeremiah put it, "I have loved you with an everlasting love; therefore I have continued my faithfulness to you." [3]

Here is grace preceding the gospel—the voice crying in the wilderness with promises of hope and renewal even in the midst of darkness. It is the voice of One nearer than our own voice *through whom* and *in whom* we are awakened unto life again.

GOD MANIFEST

God manifest! This is the event in eternity which our whole life in church is meant to proclaim: He "who for us men and for our salvation came down from heaven." The heart of the Christian message is that the Lord who "inhabiteth eternity" has acted in history—has acted in our time—to save and to redeem. That event which is a continuing action transforms and transfigures our time *insofar* as we participate in it. It yields the gift of new life and new meaning to all who see their own lost identity now in the light of God's redeeming action. The straggler in the desert or the sailor groping in the impenetrable night are lost because there is no *there*, no beacon light that calls them home. But the gospel proclaims that He who inhabits eternity has entered our aimless and fugitive time, to make it his own. His action surrounds our desert groping while we are yet a far distance away. He is the star of our night who transforms our lost direction into a purposeful journey. But his abiding is a compass that is something more than a fixed beacon. He becomes the living personal center of our renewed existence *when* we respond to his action as both judgment upon our scatteredness and as grace beyond our loveless ways.

We are like that naked (and therefore transparent) figure whom Abner Dean pictures in one of his cartoons. He is sprawled helplessly on the side of a black rock and above a chasm. Below, these words appear: "Will someone please page the three wise men!" We are the kind of creatures who are forever getting ourselves extended and helpless over the abyss of existence—never having learned to "let go" or to "trust God" because we've really never *heard* that this is the predicament to which the gospel speaks.

God manifest! This is the content and the meaning of the trinitarian affirmation of our faith. The God revealed in Christ is *one* with the Lord of eternity and the holy hidden Presence who tabernacles with us in our sacred life together. Charles Williams once said that "repentance is nothing more than a passionate intention to know all things after the mode of heaven." The season of Trinity both as an affirmation of faith and as a summary of the Christian Year—of Advent, Nativity, and Epiphany, of Crucifixion, Resurrection, Ascension, and the Coming of the Holy Spirit—is but another instance of that passionate intention to view all things after the mode of heaven. As persons we are shaped by the primary modes of our existence; and as Christians our vocation becomes one of discovering the deeper modes of heaven in our own being and becoming. In the words of the First Epistle of John, ". . . as he is, so are we in this world." [4] And again we sing in one of the ancient hymns of the church:

> O love how deep, how broad, how high,
> How passing thought and fantasy,
> That God, the Son of God, should take
> Our mortal form for mortal's sake. [5]

The roots of our identity are firmly grounded in the modes of the Trinity, for, "as he is so are we in this world."

God manifest! Certainly the first word which must be said about the God revealed in biblical history is a word which affirms both his oneness and his sovereignty. "Hear, O Israel: the Lord our God is one Lord." (Some scholars prefer the rendition, "Hear, O Israel, the Lord is our God, the Lord alone.") These are the first words of the new day on the lips of every pious Hebrew; and they are no less important for the Christian. God's sovereignty is the precondition of every other statement that we can make about our world—its stability and our integrity, its creativity and our freedom, its unexpected goodness and the mystery of our renewal.

An old Jewish legend has it that Satan was once asked what he missed most after his banishment from heaven. *"The trumpets in the morning!"* he replied. To know God is to know something of the "infinite majesty and the solemn mystery of the heavens," as James Muilenburg has written. It is to know in those unforgettable words from Job that He alone "sits above the circle of the earth," while

> the northern skies he spreads o'er empty space,
> and hangs the earth on nothing.[6]

But God is more than sheer power. He is One as each of us is one. G. Ernest Wright in his essay on "The Identity of God" (based on Isaiah 40 and 41) says that there is one thing above all else to be said about the God of the Bible. He is no "diffuse substance, idea or process." He is the "Definite One"![7] It is from the depths of God as person that we are summoned as persons. Insofar as the mode of heaven is known by man in its fullness, it is known as personal—one whose name and voice are clothed in personal acts. He is truth in person who confronts us at every juncture of life. He is the bearer of an already existing future requiring only our signature of response. He is the gracious host whose banquet is open to us—even after our paltry excuses. Surely we are judged by his grace and saved by his faithfulness.

THE MODE OF HEAVEN IN ACTION

Having confessed the all-embracing sovereignty and oneness of God we are free to turn to the diversity of his mode. I take it that the church is saying to us that the Holy Trinity as the mode of heaven is always and everywhere manifest when God confronts man. It is present with compelling intensity in the New Testament portrait of Jesus as he encountered humanity. Three occasions chosen at random from the Gospel of John may illustrate this mode:

• Jesus is speaking to those who were infuriated by his act of healing on the Sabbath. "My Father is working still," Jesus answered, "and I am working." Aside from the implication that the Sabbath was made for man and not man for the Sabbath, Jesus expresses here the primary mode of *creativity*. His opponents rightly inferred that Jesus intended not only to break the Sabbath but also to claim equality with God in the sharing of work. Indeed, the capacity for shaping and forming the materials of creation into a whole which possesses an integrity of its own, is one of the marks of God in man which point to his own creation in the image of God. Berdyaev has called creativeness "the eighth day of creation."

Work in the sense of creative response to the deep things which God has planted in his own creation is one of the primary means by which man fulfills his humanity. It is to *remember*. Has not Gibran said that remembrance is a form of meeting? It is to remember grace-inviting grace—*in* and *beyond* judgment. God's word is always nearer than the sound of our own voice, according to the author of Deuteronomy.[8] Indeed Eckhart has put it even more strikingly: "I see God with the same eye with which God sees me."

As the mode of heaven this manner of God's revelation says something even more important than work. It is saying that God invests himself in what he does, becomes, so to speak, what he does. The God of the Bible is identified primarily in his actions—not in philosophic abstraction. Theology is emphasizing today that Christ *is* what Christ *does*. In the Bible the only answer ever given to the question of God's being is to be found upon entering into his actions, that is, his saving work in history and becoming therein a participant in his work.

• Again, Jesus is replying to the insistent question of Philip, who demanded to be shown the Father. And Jesus said, "He who has seen me has seen the Father." Like another woman in Samaria—and a host of Jacobs in all the alien lands of history who complain of God-forsakenness—the Lord was in that place and Philip knew it not. The trouble with Philip, as with so many of us, was that his eyes were not for beholding—nor for perceiving the living, immediate concreteness of God.

The word becomes flesh, and the incarnation is a mode of revelation which warrants our taking seriously and reverently the givenness of creation. As Robert Frost put it, God's descent into our flesh is a demonstration that supreme merit

> Lay in risking spirit
> In substantiation.

William Blake said it in another way when he wrote, "Eternity is in love with the productions of time."

To love God, then, is to love him in his creation—in his unlovely ones as well as the lovable, in the embarrassed, the hurt, and the ugly—yea to love him even in those who hate us. For here our love becomes the means of our participation in the mode of heaven and we are reminded by Martin Buber that "creation is not a hurdle in the road of God, it is the road itself." The Incarnation as the event of Christ is only begun in the Nativity. It is the action through which God renews and continues creation. It is God, our Father, at work and our entering into his labor through participation in the event:

> How shall we love Thee, holy hidden Being
> If we love not the world which Thou hast made?
> O give us brother-love for better seeing
> Thy word made flesh, and in a manger laid.[9]

• The final incident reflects the work of the spirit in the community of faith. Nicodemus, that sophisticated man of learning, respects the results of Christ's preaching but is scandalized by the means. "Unless one is born of water and the Spirit," we hear him repeating distastefully, "he cannot enter the kingdom of God?" These are difficult words for one who wants to remain aloof and secure in his own knowledge.

Baptism is the sacrament of this new birth and its cost is measured in the degree to which one is willing to be buried with Christ in his death in order that one may be raised with him in his resurrection. We are strangers to such sacrifice. We are afraid of demands so deep that we can meet them only by a corresponding act of birth—afraid and suspicious! So we turn away from such demands and content ourselves with a rehearsal of our own excuses—begging, meanwhile, to remain unencumbered by embarrassing promises. Our hearts are hardened, our eyes become heavy, and our ears are too fat to hear, while

> . . . a ragged urchin, aimless and alone,
> Loitered about that vacancy, a bird
> Flew up to safety from his well-aimed stone:
> That girls are raped, that two boys knife a third,
> Were axioms to him who'd never heard
> Of any world where promises were kept,
> Or one could weep because another wept. . . .[10]

The mode of heaven awaits our response before that vacancy shall be filled with *promises that are kept.*

THE LIVING HOPE KEPT IN HEAVEN

So God's manifestation by the modes of heaven becomes the means whereby we are gathered—as the church and as persons. In that meeting and in its living remembrance we, too, are a gathered unity. The mode of heaven is the basis of our integrity, for we are persons after the mode of heaven. "Thy years are one day," wrote Augustine as he addressed a prayer to God, "and thy day is not every day but today; because thy today neither gives place to tomorrow nor comes it in place of yesterday. Thy today is eternity."

The living hope which is the inheritance of those who know Christ in his resurrection *is kept in heaven*. It is a trust which, though it constantly is revealed in human action, is never wiped out in human failure. It is kept in heaven but in God's time "today is eternity." Every day, indeed every new beginning, is the day of salvation. In the moment, *now,* before us, we may "cash in" on our inheritance kept in heaven.

It is in relation to our transcendent God, then, that we are able to affirm our own transcendent personhood now—beyond "the perpetual perishings of time." We can neither possess nor guarantee that transcendency by our own effort; it is the gift which comes of entering into and becoming a part of God's gracious events in history. But there are two corresponding modes of human existence which are surely near the heart of heaven. They are laughter and gratitude. Despite our earth-boundness, wherever these expressions of human transcendence are present there is good cause to hope that we live not *far from the Kingdom*—and under the aspect of eternity.

We are persons after the mode of heaven, and the mode of heaven is revealed ever anew in this amazing grace,

> That God, the son of God, should take
> Our mortal form for mortal's sake.

• *Notes for Chapter 5*

1. I Peter 1:3-4.

2. Quoted from an article "Master Conversationalist at Work" by John Ciardi who reported an interview with Frost in *The Saturday Review*, March 21, 1959. The fragment is from "Kitty Hawk" in the book of poems by Robert Frost titled *In the Clearing* (New York: Holt, Rinehart and Winston, Inc., copyright © 1956, 1962). Used by permission of the publisher.

3. Jeremiah 31:3.

4. I John IV (BCP).

5. Latin, 15th century.

6. Job 26:7 (Moffatt).

7. "The Identity of God," in *The Rule of God* (Philadelphia: The Westminster Press, 1959).

8. See Deuteronomy, Ch. 30.

9. John Houseman, 1919. *The Hymnal 1940* (New York: The Church Pension Fund, 1940), No. 112.

10. W. H. Auden, "The Shield of Achilles," *The Collected Poetry of W. H. Auden* (New York: Random House, Inc., Modern Library, 1959), p. 136. Used by permission.

6: Eternity in Person

&s§ But when the time had fully come, God sent forth his Son, born of woman, born under the law, to redeem those who were under the law, so that we might receive adoption as sons. . . .[1]

EARLIER we referred to W. H. Auden's play, "For the Time Being," which is a fleeting glimpse of our unrehearsed encounter each year with the meaning behind the birth of Christ. These words from the postlogue of that play are apt to linger on in our disturbed conscience:

> To those who have seen
>   The Child,
> however dimly, however incredulously,
> The Time Being is, in a sense, the most trying
>   time of all. . . .
> Remembering the stable where for once in our
>   lives
> Everything became a you and nothing was an
>   IT. . . .[2]

On the other hand, the text from Galatians above reflects the conviction of the early church: that Jesus is the Christ who in the fullness of time has come to claim us in kindredness and love. Somewhere between that conviction of the church and our wistful celebration of the event we have lost contact with the new creation which God wrought in Jesus Christ. And perhaps just because it is so painful by contrast we prefer to keep Christ in a precious Disneyland of make-believe, in order to protect ourselves from the Christ who in setting his time over against our time reveals our emptiness and our death.

For the spirit which inhabits our time is not the spirit of love which lives by losing its life for the sake of the brethren. It assumes a defensive posture, it holds fast to what it imagines it can possess and too often it accounts time not to "praise God and to enjoy him forever," but as a burden to be paced off into insignificance. That picture of Satan at the beginning of the book of Job is an accurate portrayal of this age; a restless, aimless, "no-body" wandering "to and fro," "up and down," in the earth. Here is the contagion of this age, wherever men gather—life lived under the aspect of the "8:15"!

WHAT IS MAN?

What is man? To ask the question is to suggest that man is a creature who always bears the knowledge that he is not what he was intended to be. He was made as the seal of perfection, according to Ezekiel, ". . . full of wisdom and perfect in beauty . . . till iniquity was found in thee." [3] Despite our dreams for man, it is this conviction that we have not fulfilled our promise, have not entered into our inheritance as sons, which, in its distorted way, sends us in a never-ending, fever-driven search for our own lost cities of promise. Tennessee Williams puts it in these words from the mouth of Big Daddy in "Cat on a Hot Tin Roof":

> . . . the human animal is a beast that dies and if he's got money he buys and buys and buys and I think the reason he buys everything he can buy is that in the back of his mind he has the crazy hope that one of his purchases will be life everlasting.[4]

Again, one may say that the human animal is a creature who looks for a Messiah—but never recognizes his coming! He usually settles for a sorcerer instead. Are we not all represented in that band of John's disciples who met Christ with the question, "Art thou he that should come or do we look for another?" To adapt some words of Santayana, in the presence of such yearning for magic, one is always tempted to promise more than he can deliver! And, if that question is addressed to the politician or a doctor, or even a preacher, who, like Barkis, "is willin'," we are likely to discover anew just how intoxicating the temptation to idolatry is—and how habit forming!

What is man? Mostly he is a creature who waits and endures. Even though tyranny would crush his individuality, and the world of the "8:15" with its ever-increasing production line, its economically monitored, one-way communication, and its standardized product, would reduce his stature to something much lower than the angels—man may falter but he endures. The endurance of the poor is unnerving. Here endurance is a kind of waiting in divine discontent—a discontent that often saves us. Listen: "My soul waiteth for the Lord, more than they who watch for the morning." How long has it been since you have waited for the morning—searching the retreating night for some ray of hope? Such long nights yield their own kind of "happy issue" out of affliction. I am suggesting that even when man is in the depth of despair, there is a watchfulness and expectancy about the human spirit that is always prompted to look for God's coming, ". . . more than they who watch for the morning! And the deeper reality beyond that watchfulness is the profound knowledge that man was meant for a relation to God—and nothing else will satisfy his passion. Apart from God his soul is twisted and cramped by anxiety, and he is obsessed with one question, Why? Why? Why?

This is man. And God was made man in Christ: *Born of a woman, born under the law, crucified under Pontius Pilate, dead and buried!* Does that make it concrete enough? Paul adds that he emptied himself and, also, that God even made him to be sin for us—him, who knew no sin. It is precisely into this world where man in his headlong attempt to escape God has crowded out Eternity, that God comes again in the fullness of time. He is eternity in person. He invades our time with love: he confronts our time with eternity, our possessiveness with his gift, our squandered years driven before the vengeance of busyness, with the effortlessness of his creation. He even restores the days and nights for the telling of his glory. But, most disturbing of all, he reveals our inmost selves. His is the mirror of grace which reflects the fact that we prefer to be the sons of Cain and that we go on murdering our brother in one way or another until we see Christ also reflected as healing our wounds before we seek help. We are saved by the *exceptions* of God—by sheer unmerited gift; and Christ is the supreme instance of grace where, in love beyond our sin, we encounter God who claims us as his own. This is our "unspeakable" gift in Christ.

WHO IS CHRIST?

That God was made man in Christ lays emphasis upon the fact that God is always and wholly personal. It is only by personal acts that we have living knowledge of God—never in abstract propositions. Therefore God's action in Christ is a way of confirming his identity and, through him, our own. It is of the nature of God that when he becomes man he becomes man in Jesus Christ. One mode of revelation points to the other. And it is of the nature of man's relation to God in Jesus Christ that when he discovers and appropriates that relation, his integrity, his freedom, and his identity are affirmed as in no other way.

• As Lord of time and space God sends his son to redeem our time and space. Apart from God, as we have seen, our existence is constantly being reduced to nothingness. It is a sobering thought to realize that left to ourselves, our relation to one another tends to be a mutually destructive one. "If all hearts were open and all desires known," Thomas Hardy once wrote, "how many gapings, sighings, clenched fists, knotted brows, broad grins and red eyes would we see in the market place." This is a thought which reminds us of Sartre's thesis in "No Exit," that we cannot live in proximity to one another without clawing and tearing each other apart.

But as the One who redeems time Christ is both the *parousia* (the future already present) and the *telos* (the end) in our time. He is the flowering of humanity—his person is the bearer of God's intention for man from the beginning. In Christ every moment points beyond itself while it is itself transformed. We know this truth profoundly in great Christian music—in the chorales of Bach, the "Messiah" of Handel, Luther's "Cradle Song," and in the Negro spiritual. Christ is eternity in person: and *in faith* every person participates in his eternity.

• As the Father of our Lord Jesus Christ, God sends his son to claim that which he has loved from eternity. "I have chosen thee": this profound conviction of the Hebrews, the occasion of their unending song—this love toward us men from everlasting to everlasting—became man in Jesus Christ. "I have chosen thee": this is the meaning of Christ's coming; and the song is transmuted into a great joy occasioned by the event in which the word becomes flesh and we are enabled to behold his glory full of beauty and truth. The significance of Jesus Christ is communicated in the fact that he chose us. It is that choice which constitutes our personhood. False gods cannot choose. Rather they are chosen—and usually as a last desperate gamble, at that!

WE ARE MET AS PERSONS IN CHRIST

The God who seeks us in the person of Jesus Christ reveals to us both his mind and his heart which cannot be less than personal. Only in the wake of such love are we able to forget or to lay aside our self-centered universe. Is not this the significance of the Good Samaritan? He forgot himself and laid aside every prior claim —even religious prohibitions regarding traffic with aliens as he was caught up in the desperate need of another human being. Could we not say that Christ is the source of that response as well as its object? For Christ is also the broken man left in the ditch to die, whom we encounter on our busy journeys from Jerusalem down to Jericho! This is the scandal of the gospel. It betrays our helplessness in the very moment that it reveals Christ. "You think you hate your enemy," Augustine reminds us, "when it is Christ whom you hate."

Wherever the response of love is *given* and *received* there also is Christ. To know Christ is to know something of the Father's love who sent him forth to claim us again as sons. As we respond to that love we are enabled to hear with our ears, and to see with our eyes and to touch with our hands *as if for the first time*. All things become new in the presence of such love. Christ himself is the first fruit of the new creation.

This nascent life which is ours in Christ is ours as a gift. In him we discover the One who, as the Book of Common Prayer expresses it, is "more ready to hear than we to pray." It is this "for-giveness" which engenders repentance in us that serves as a fulcrum, turning wrath into grace. The gospel is gift restoring and renewing life. Perhaps this is what Charles Williams had in mind when he wrote those words concerning Mary, the Mother of Jesus. Joseph says in the play, "Grab and Grace," "She is the manifest measure of God's glory correcting time."

To be a person is to know oneself in relation to time and eternity. In Christ we claim our relation to the whole of creation through faith. Faith is personal response to God's action as person. It is to respond to God's eternity whom we know in the person, Jesus Christ. "Faith alone," writes Emil Brunner, "knows the mystery of the person or the authority of the Revealer."

• *Notes for Chapter 6*

1. Galatians 4:4-5.
2. *The Collected Poetry of W. H. Auden* (New York: Random House, Inc., 1945), pp. 465-466.
3. Ezekiel 28:12, 15.
4. Tennessee Williams, "Cat on a Hot Tin Roof" (New York: New Directions, 1955), p. 73. Reprinted by permission of New Directions, Publishers.

7: God with Us

And I will pray the Father, and he shall give you another Comforter, that he may abide with you forever.[1]

"How can i explain 'hell' to my child," one baffled parent asks. My answer is that one does not need to "explain" it. One has only to open his eyes as did the prodigal son and find himself already there. The child may be understandably frightened and unduly disturbed by a hell that is beyond his experience; but we are deceiving ourselves if we refuse to acknowledge that the youngster who knows how to use every human need as a tool, and even as a weapon, has not also experienced the equivalent of what we call hell. One can hardly read J. D. Salinger's novel[2] about a "crazy mixed-up kid" called Holden Caulfield without becoming a little more informed, if not disturbed, about the penetrating frankness and sophistication of young people. On one occasion Holden asked his pious schoolmate if he thought that Christ would have sent Judas, the betrayer, to hell. When he received an affirmative answer, Holden objected, "I can't believe that Christ would have sent old Judas to hell, but any one of those

damn disciples would have!" Holden Caulfield would
not need to have hell explained. His deeper perplexity
is how people who call themselves "Christian" keep on
sending each other there.

HELL: OUR CONTEMPORARY

Another way of looking at the reality of hell is to say
that Christ is on the Cross as long as there is a sinner
in hell; and we know that our history has been a continual crucifixion. In the Middle Ages, Dante peopled
his hell with contemporary figures and familiar his-
torical characters. It is important to remember that
"The Divine Comedy" always has its hell in contemporary form. Hell is too real to be relegated to costume
drama.

To be sure, there is one common element in every
hell. It is the prevailing spirit, the tyranny of mind
which is dominated by anxious self-centeredness. It is
demon possession in the form of a consuming anxiety
to encompass all things which, at the same time, renders
the person unable either to receive or to give love.
Isaiah speaks of Sheol (Hell) as having "enlarged its
appetite and opened its mouth beyond measure." [3] Hell
is life lived under the engrossing drive to view all
things, *not* after the mode of heaven *but* in the shadow
of a dark idolatry of the self. The writer of Ecclesiastes
must have known what it is to live in hell. A few terse
sentences describe his course: "Come now, I will make
a test of pleasure; enjoy yourself. . . . But . . . what use
is it? . . . I made great works. . . . Then I considered all
that my hands had done and the toil I had spent in

doing it, and behold all was vanity and a striving after wind. . . . So I turned my heart over to despair. . . ." [4] Who has not touched this course at some point in a generation of angry young men? Actually we are in hell when in all things we have our own way! Nor will God deny us that freedom which apart from him becomes slavery in hell.

But hell is not only a prevailing spirit. It is also a destination. It is life turned in the direction of death rather than life. It becomes the abode of damnation where people prefer lies to truth, deceit before honesty, and a chasm of loneliness rather than a relationship of trust. No scene in modern fiction is more expressive of a life and a living that is damned "from here to eternity" than the final pages of the novel which uses that phrase as a title. Two women stand at the rail as their boat leaves Honolulu harbor; and each miserably lost and spent soul lies to the other, each knowing that the other is lying!

THE HOLY SPIRIT: GOD WITH US

The promise of God also involves spirit and an abode. It proposes to renovate hell with the living, renewing presence of none other than God himself as Holy Spirit. One of the prevailing pictures of this hell-breaker in the Gospel is that of the Good Shepherd who is forever seeking the scattered sheep who have wandered and strayed. And the music of heaven, according to the New Testament, is the sound of joy when even one lost in hell is brought home again. Despite the ordeal of the first centuries and their persecutions this image is the most characteristic scene of the early art in the Christian church.

The inner meaning of hell is death in the midst of life. The gift of God's abiding spirit is eternal life. These alternatives—life or death—confront us across the span of days. Both are "live options" in every moment of existence. And it is always important to be testing the spirit by which one lives (not every spirit is holy, nor all prayer worthy, just as mere religion is not enough). There used to be a profoundly moving sermon on the subject of "trains" given by an old Negro preacher which has relevance for all of us. One of his trains was called "The Black Diamond Express." "It runs between here and hell," he would explain, "making thirteen stops and always arriving in hell ahead of schedule." And those who "need no repentance," we might add, are always arriving in hell ahead of themselves.

God the Holy Spirit refers to the third mode of the Trinity by which the Divine is known to us and in response to which we participate in Eternity. He is "the Lord and Giver of Life, who proceedeth from the Father and the Son; who with the Father and the Son together is worshiped and glorified; who spake by the prophets." Put another way, Christ said simply: "I will not leave you comfortless: I will come to you."

We must not let this word *comfort* mislead us. The Greek word is *Paraclete*. The author of the Fourth Gospel used it deliberately to portray the new, abiding presence of God as Holy Spirit in the community of the faithful. In 1611 when the translators of the King James Version looked around for an equivalent word they hit upon *comfort* which for them had something of Luther's martial strain in it,

> A mighty fortress is our God,
> A bulwark never failing.

Indeed the root meaning of *con* and *fortare* suggesting the strength of a fortress is still there, but it must be admitted that the word comfort suggests something soft to us—just the opposite of firm and strengthening presence.

We have said that the promise of the gospel is both a spirit and a destination. It is God as Spirit to whom man as spirit is able to respond—even from behind the iron curtain of hell. Indeed, it is this deep calling unto deep which disturbs our waking hours with heavenly discontent and overtakes us in our flight with the reminder that we were meant for a heavenly discourse. As long as that voice is there man can never be satisfied with himself as a mere bundle of reflexes whose meaning is exhausted by some measuring rod. Daniel Day Williams has put it thus: "Man is spirit. He is a free creative participant in the process of becoming. Spirit is our name for personality in action, encountering and responding to the demands of life." And the indwelling Spirit is *paraclete* or advocate in the sense of unwavering help within the church. There, He is the giver of life who draws the faithful with loving cords toward all truth while becoming the means whereby all that the Father has done is recollected and represented in the actional life of the church. By that indwelling and consequently transfigured life the church is enabled, and its people empowered, to reclaim their adoption as sons of God—to become what they already are. As Luther once said in his summary of the Trinity: "To the Father we ascribe the work of creation; to the Son the work of Redemption; to the Holy Spirit the power to forgive sins, to gladden, to strengthen, to transport from death to eternal life."

SPIRIT AND CHURCH

One of the early Fathers of the church declared, "I believe in the Holy Spirit and the Holy Church." There is a direct and necessary relation between the Spirit and the community which lives by the Spirit. Indeed, one way of defining the church is to say that the church is where the Spirit is Lord: and the gates of hell shall not prevail against it. The Spirit is the vitality of the church—its life. There He is known as nowhere else. There in the community gathered by the Spirit the fruits of the Christian life are known in their fullness— love, joy, peace, and the like. The Psalmist expressed this view of the church long before Christianity came on the scene, "The angel of the Lord encamps around those who fear him, and delivers them." [5]

There is a profound relation between the coming of the Spirit and the pains of new birth. Perhaps it is here that we need to understand the analogies which have been used to explain the relation of Christ to the church. It has been called the Body of Christ and the Bride of Christ. In each case the analogy emphasizes the fact that one's entry into that union betwixt Christ and his church is always something like a birth—with its pain and its joy. Lincoln was profoundly aware of

this truth in the moment when he called for a new birth
of freedom under God.

That discipline is present *first* of all as we test the
Spirit—and find that this Spirit judges our own in that
it gives itself for the brethren. In our effort to insulate
and protect ourselves "from the contagion of the world's
slow stain" we suffocate any new life—new mission—
which could enter and transform our tight little world.
It is only in moments of painfully transparent insight
that we see ourselves as we really are—standing in need
of an Advocate to save and renew. It is not merely in-
cidental that a yoke is one of the symbols of Christianity. Its acceptance bears the additional reminder that
a yoke is also an instrument of shared work. Paul in
Philippians appeals to Euodia and Syntyche to put aside
their conflict and to agree in the Lord. And he directs
another "comrade" *in the same yoke* to act as inter-
mediary. Christ from the heart of the Eucharist offers
his yoke to the beloved. And if the mode of Christ's
work leads in the same direction of self-emptying, can
we ask any more than those first Christians for whom
Paul left this memorial?

> We are afflicted in every way but not crushed;
> perplexed but not driven to despair;
> struck down but not destroyed;
> always carrying in the body the death of Jesus,
> so that the life of Jesus may also be manifested
>   in our bodies. . . .[6]

Second, worship in the community where the Spirit
is Lord is always under the discipline of truth. Its openness is an openness to new truth and new birth. One of

the dangers of the church with which God as Holy
Spirit must continually struggle is the tendency of the
church to idolatrize itself and to reduce personal and
dynamic truth to abstract, freedom-destroying formulae. The prophetic witness of God as Holy Spirit calls
into question every confessional statement. It is not
strange, then, that the church which lives by a continual recalling of the mighty action of God, finds it
dangerous to define too closely just how that event
saves. God's grace is not restricted by man's effort to
describe it. God as Holy Spirit abides with the church—
but as judgment as well as grace. That is the charter of
the church's renewal.

The church, then, which is brought to life by the
Holy Spirit, is the locus, the place where saints live in
communion, sins are forgiven, the body is resurrected
beyond death, and life is eternal. It is the community
of faith which overcomes despair. It is the community
wherein all things are *remembered (anamnesis)*—the
manifest measure of God's glory correcting time. Here
one is *enabled* to become a person after the mode of
heaven—a partner with God in the dialogue of time.
Here history becomes history *in Christ,* and time is recovered and redirected by its *telos* in the Holy Spirit
just as space is recovered and consecrated by his *parousia* in the church. And here also we know the full meaning of his word by the prophet,

> "I am the first and I am the last:
>   besides me there is no god."

• *Notes for Chapter 7*

1. John 14:16 (KJV).
2. *The Catcher in the Rye* (New York: New American Library, 1953; original publishers, Little, Brown & Co., 1945).
3. Isaiah 5:14.
4. Ecclesiastes 2:1,2,4,11,20, in part.
5. Psalm 34:7.
6. II Corinthians 4:8-10.
7. Isaiah 44:6.

8: The Church and Our Identity

✑ Beloved, we are God's children now. . . .[1]

IN ONE of his most striking passages G. K. Chesterton writes,

> We have all forgotten who we really are. All that we call common sense and rationality and practicality and positivism only means that for certain dead levels of life we forget that we have forgotten. All that we call spirit and art and ecstasy only means that for one awful instant we remember that we forget.[2]

The Christian is reminded that his identity is rooted in his relation to God symbolized by that invisible cross which the church has placed on his forehead. All that we do in church is meant to be a reminder of who we are: "Beloved, we are God's children now. . . ."

To forget who we are, or to be forgotten, is another way of experiencing death in the midst of life. This is the nothingness—the emptiness—of life apart from the creative action of God. To be a person is to belong to some enduring community. Man cannot long survive separation from those deep roots in a community from

95

which his identity is derived nor from that self-transcendence which his community of faith affords in its capacity to judge every organization in the light of God's truth. But, as Allen Wheelis the psychiatrist has pointed out, contemporary man faces the terrible dilemma that if he identifies himself with certain values and their perpetuation he is apt to find himself also out of touch and irrelevant to his own time. If, on the other hand, he takes his values from the changing tide of public taste he suffers the loss of his self. "Not knowing what he stands for," writes Wheelis, "he does not know who he is." [3]

His lost identity is the spur which compels a man to keep on searching. Somewhere in the dark one is met by God. His grace anticipates our aimless journey—awaiting a ready heart. God continues to will creation *ex nihilo*—to seek and to recover man from the wastelands of his own making. Indeed, Christ on the cross is the measure of that unceasing quest and that grace which is forever making man *new* beyond the abyss of his own nothingness. God the Eternal enters man's history in the event of Christ and through his response in faith man is woven back into the pattern of eternity. Insofar as he participates in this event in eternity, which is also an event in time, man is restored to himself—restored to an identity which is transcendent to the vicissitudes of time. "And this is eternal life," says Christ in that Johannine prayer, "that they know thee the only true God, and Jesus Christ whom thou hast sent."

THE CHURCH AS RESPONSE

All that we have been saying thus far about the church and the person is caught up in these words from the poet, Rilke: "The future enters into us," he writes, "in order to transform itself in us, long before it happens." So far we have been concerned with the modes of God's prior coming into our lives. Now we shall turn to the modes of our response and the conditions which are necessary for our appropriation of the fruits of the spirit. Indeed, the church itself, and its life as the congregation of Christ's flock, is the result of both the mode of heaven and of man's response as he finds himself in that life. As Emil Brunner has pointed out, the church comes into being only because the apostle comes from his transfiguring encounter with God and gives to others what he himself has received. The church is "built upon the foundation of the apostles and prophets." "The existence of the church," Brunner writes, "is based upon this apostolic act of turning toward man. . . ."

When the pagans taunted the early Christians by accusing them of worshiping a dead God, Athanasius flung back the challenge: "How, then, is it," he countered, "that He makes the wicked cease from his wickedness, the murderer from murder, the unjust from avarice. . . . Oh, no," Athanasius concluded, "it is he [Christ] himself who brought death to naught and daily raises monuments to his own disciples." [4]

We dare not claim with the boldness of an Athanasius that we who bear the mark of discipleship in this day are "monuments to Christ's victory." But we do confess that the identical power of God is at work in our midst and that we live by the promise of that power authenticating itself in us and in the work of the church. Indeed, the church as it fulfills the promise of the Gospel is the means whereby the undergirding identity of God is extended in his people. "We know that we have passed out of death into life," wrote our Johannine chronicler, "because we love the brethren." [5] And even more, we might add in the same spirit, *because we know ourselves to be the sons of God*.

THE CHURCH AND THE CONDITION OF PERSONHOOD

To abide in Christ is to accept our responsible relation to one another in this community which his Spirit has called into existence. It is a community which springs *not* from human effort but from repentance, forgiveness, and from a steadfast continuing "in the apostle's doctrine and fellowship, and in the breaking of bread and prayer." The church, then, is not merely an assembly of high-minded people. It is not an enchanted garden provided for those who only want to deny evil, or to shut out suffering, or to keep their hands unsullied from a dirty world. It is set in the midst of this world of cabbages and kings, of battle, murder, and sudden death. Nor is the church an ecclesiastical world set against this wicked world just as heaven is not a parson's paradise where all people eventually have to be good! The church is man's true home where, as in Robert Frost's poem, one does not have to *deserve* in order to *belong*.

It is not enough to say that the existence of the

person implies the existence of a genuine community, although the two are intimately related. To be a person implies a special kind of community. *First,* it must be a community that affords face-to-face meeting—small enough and "in touch" enough to call out the intimacy of the person. Too often the real person is lost in our large congregations. A. D. Lindsay believes that small face-to-face groups, such as in the family, the church, and labor unions, are the necessary foundations of a free society. *Second,* community must afford social proximity *and* social distance, both of which are necessary for the person's development and integrity. We become persons in relation to the opposition as well as to the acceptance of others. "A good marriage," as Rilke has expressed it, "is one in which each appoints the other guardian of his solitude." *Third,* a freedom-bestowing community is one that requires no more conformity than is necessary for its own existence. Genuine community is based on the conviction that every human organization must be judged in relation to the freedom and integrity which it affords the person.

Now when we look for these conditions in our secular world we are hard pressed to find them. Can they exist apart from religious conviction? Lord Acton, the English historian, has said that the concept of freedom, as we know it in our civilization, rests upon the Hebrew-Christian conviction of an area of inviolate freedom at the heart of every person—which is exempt from the power of the state. The same must be said of every primary group which nurtures the person. Its health depends upon its capacity to sustain creative criticism and prophetic judgment within its own ranks. If it stills the voice of the prophet and retreats from every suggestion of change, it has forfeited its capacity to nurture free men. Indeed, it is already dead.

It is precisely this creative tension which is the mark of the church. It is by grace, by the love of God, by the indwelling of the Holy Spirit that an ordinary group is transformed into a community of persons. By the same indwelling the person and the community live in dynamic tension; for man's identity in church is defined by the relation of the gospel as *Kerygma,* to the church as *Koinonia.* Thus, every Christian is a living witness to the health or sickness of the church as a renewing community of faith.

THE EARTHLY REALITY OF THE CHURCH

The church is our common life in the Body of Christ. John Knox, the New Testament scholar, has written:

> The church is the community which came into being with the event (of Christ) and in which the event in its totality occurred. . . . It is the community in which alone the life, death and resurrection of Christ as a *revelatory event* took place.[6]

As the locus, the place, which intends to become all that the gospel proclaims, the church binds us together in "one body" which is like that in marriage. Indeed, we are to become one flesh and one body with Christ. Are you surprised, then, that the early Christians regarded any unnecessary absence from that body in its liturgical action as a fracture of the body of Christ? Is an arm still an arm apart from the body which is its whole? So the individual Christian possesses his vital life only within and as a part of his participation in the spirit-filled community.

The corporeality of the church means that Christ redeems not only time but also the world of space. Another way of saying this is that when the word became flesh in Christ, all things were made sacred in principle. The church indwelt by the Holy Spirit moves in the direction of a world made holy by his presence. His redemption includes our bodies as well as our spirit. Indeed, he has set in motion the power that will not rest until

> . . . the earth shall be filled with the glory of God
> As the waters cover the sea.

The church is a corporate reality but its manifestation according to Paul "is not in word but in power." Modern man does not lack knowledge of what he ought to do. His life is burdened with an uneasy conscience under the weight of grievous and tyrannical oughts. He knows abundantly what he ought to do. What he lacks is the power to do. When John the Baptist's emissaries came inquiring of Jesus if he were the Messiah, Christ's answer was not in word but in power. "Go and tell John what you hear and see," he answered.

> The blind receive their sight
> And the lame walk,
> Lepers are cleansed,
> And the deaf hear
> And the dead are raised up,
> And the poor have good news
> preached to them.[7]

It was this power as well as word which made the Christian church a home for saints and a living embodiment of the unity of truth and community, of person and identity. But the secret of that new reality and its enabling power comes from the fact that it is a community organized not in terms of some ideal but in relation to the living person and event of Christ. Its life is based upon remembrance—a continuing rehearsal of man's deepest identity—not upon mere striving. Just as God's relation to man is deep calling unto deep, so Christ's relation to his church is personal event related to personal event. In church the event of Christ becomes our event. One of the Great Reformers, Melanchthon, declared, "The Kingdom of Christ is to know his benefits, taste his salvation and experience his grace."

THE CHURCH LIVES BY MISSION

Our final word is that the church in which we discover our true identity lives by mission as a fire exists by burning. It is not a mutual protection society but a home base for saints on a holy mission of love and self-sacrifice in response to the gift of God.

The end and purpose of the church is not a doctrine, nor a moral code, nor even a satisfying philosophy of life. It is a person—a person in his recovered identity under God. In Proverbs 16:4 we read, "The Lord hath made all things for himself. . . ." The scholars tell us that this verse could also be translated, "The Lord hath made all things for their own purpose." Man's "own purpose" is fulfilled only in relation to God whose intention from creation is not only that he *be* but also that he be freely and fully personal.

The person lives by response and commitment. One is a person *only* in relation to another person. Neither doctrine nor moral codes nor intellectual propositions can give life to the person. The integrity, the identity of the person is called out by the eternal love of God which is new every morning, "O Lord, Thou hast searched me and known me!"

To be known of God and to live in a community of such knowledge is to know oneself. And such personal identity is sustained only in that community whose time and space is spent not in self-ended pursuits but in self-giving and glad response to God. The structure of lives, our music, architecture—even a lamp post, as G. K. Chesterton used to say—are to become witnesses to grace. The purpose of the church then is fulfilled in becoming itself; and in that becoming we discover the full meaning of our own identity in Christ.

"Beloved, we are God's children now. . . ."

• *Notes for Chapter 8*

1. I John 3:2.
2. Reprinted by permission of Dodd, Mead & Company from *Orthodoxy* by G. K. Chesterton, 1952, pp. 96-97.
3. Allen Wheelis, *The Quest for Identity* (New York: W. W. Norton & Co., Inc., 1958), p. 129.
4. *De Incarnatione Verbi Dei*, English trans. (New York: The Macmillan Company, 1946), pp. 59 and 61.
5. I John 3:14.
6. In *Jesus Lord and Christ* (New York: Harper & Brothers, 1958), p. 222.
7. Matthew 11:5.

PART THREE 𝕭

The Occasions of Gift Giving

The church year is a continual *anamnesis* of the sacred events in which the whole Christ comes to us and draws us into participation in him.

A. T. MOLLEGEN [1]

"Did we deserve, dearest, under the law, this birth that I kiss? Nothing at all is given till all is given, I know; that is heaven. But then also it is heaven to know that all is given at once in the smallest gift—even sometimes when only half given. O my Son reckons as no arithmetician has done; he checks his suits by the least and the greatest at once. O my own, there are no, no accounts like yours."

CHARLES WILLIAMS [2]

---

[1] "Christmastide and Epiphany," in *Preaching the Christian Year*, Howard Johnson, ed. (New York: Charles Scribner's Sons, 1957).

[2] Mary, of Jesus, in "The House by the Stable," *Seed of Adam, and Other Plays* (New York: Oxford University Press, Inc., 1948).

9: Of Gifts and Gift Giving

    For by grace you have been saved through faith; and this is not your own doing, it is the gift of God. . . .[1]

SOME TIME AGO I had the privilege of baptizing a child in the Washington Cathedral. As I approached this young lady of two years, she offered me a gift—a single flower which she carried in her hand. That child's action reflects something of the profound and renewing mystery of our faith—a gift given in spontaneous trust and affection which has the power to translate an ordinary experience into the realm of redemption.

It occurs to me that this is the way the kingdom of God comes: not in striving and busyness, but as an adult receives the unmerited gift of a child's love. At the very heart of our faith, the mysterious power of gift giving is encountered. Salvation is the gift of God; it is not the product of man's anxious labor. Perhaps we could go further by saying that this motif is the heart of religion itself. It is man's numinous response to gift in the depths of his being—gift from a source which is wholly other than himself and yet strangely kin to himself. There is profound truth in the statement of

Pestalozzi that God is our nearest relative; for it is in response to him whose service is perfect freedom that we are enabled to come to ourselves—to discover and appropriate the gift of our own identity. When Paul wanted to sum up the never-before-revealed mystery of God in Christ he pointed to the fulfillment of those words familiar to every Hebrew, "When he ascended on high he led a host of captives, and he gave gifts to men." [2]

The mystery of gifts and of gift giving is the mystery which is hid from the wise and the clever but revealed to children and to the pure in heart. It is an "open" secret—accessible to all, whether found upon the lips of a St. Francis or deep in the heart of the washerwoman about whom Carl Sandburg wrote, "Rubbing underwear she sings of the Last Great Washday."

The mystery of every gift points to the hidden power of God's free gift to man. It is a liberating force the consequences of which can be neither anticipated nor controlled. But its dynamic is evidenced in the renewing fellowship of those who are able to give and to receive genuine gifts of one another. The church in *eucharist* is meant to show forth "the fellowship of the mystery" where captives to sin and anxiety are moved to give themselves anew in response to the gift of Christ. Who can measure the length and breadth of that gift in Christian history?

THE DECLINE OF GIFT GIVING

But gift giving in this day has come to mean for many something entirely different. A friend who has been engaged in research on this subject has uncovered some rather sobering facts. He has found, for instance, that in terms of the social function which it seems to serve, the practice of gift giving is one means of group control and of conformity. It tends to become an activity largely motivated by "expectations" from *without*, rather than by the spontaneous impulse to give, from *within*. Thus, when a gift is proposed among fellow workers for one who is about to leave the group, the first questions which are likely to be asked are these: "What is expected of me?" "How much should I give?" "What are others giving?" The objective observer concludes that gift giving appears to be nothing more than another way that "other-directed" men and women act out their charade of conformity. To be sure, he will admit that there could be such a thing as an uncalculated gift giving, but his method of observation has been unable to detect its presence on the social scene. For the Christian these disclosures call not for a mad scramble to prove that some residue of spontaneous gift giving, left over from robust faith, remains, but a humble acceptance of the judgment conveyed in the fact that the genuine article has practically disappeared.

The other side of this dilemma—namely, the incapacity to receive a gift—is equally disturbing. Since we have put a price on everything (including ourselves), we are more likely to shy away from all gifts for fear that we may become obligated. We have forgotten how to be gracious recipients of gifts. How many marriages—indeed, how many human relationships—flounder on this fear of love, of gifts? There is something of this fatal incapacity to trust a gift in one of the Gospel stories. Do you remember the incident when, faced with the necessity of food for the multitude, one of the disciples blurted out: "There is a lad here who has five barley loaves and two fish"? Perhaps his words reflect the enthusiastic offer of a small boy's lunch. But caution intervened. Not wishing to appear ridiculous, he added, "But what are they among so many?" [3]

What indeed! The apostles were to learn—what the world has not yet learned—that a genuine gift represents infinitely more than its weight or measure. No matter how small, when offered and shared in response to love, it becomes enlarged not merely in quantity but in graceful significance beyond human imagination. Indeed, human history is full of the remnants of saving events in which a cup of cold water administered appropriately to some "little one" has redirected human destiny.

GIFT IS THE HEART OF THE GOSPEL

Both giving and receiving are at the heart of the gospel. Gifts and gift giving are the root and structure of human community—and identity. Christ gave the gifts of relationship when he asked the woman at the well for a drink of water. In that simple request the means of communication and communion were established. Again his gift of healing was there for the asking when another pleaded. "Lord, help me!" He gave himself in the abiding community of remembrance in the breaking of bread.

Giving and receiving establishes a community in which there is the acceptance of mutual trust and de-

pendence. Perhaps this is the deeper reason why we
are afraid of gifts: to accept a gift from another is to be
drawn into a community based not on proving oneself
but on mutual forbearance and acceptance in love. We
cannot accept or love others because down deep inside
we are possessed by the conviction that we are, indeed,
unlovable and unacceptable. The simple truth that God
cared enough to give himself for us is inaccessible to
our frantic efforts to prove our worth; and we cannot
purchase heaven precisely because it is a gift. The truth
remains: the most important things in life are given.
They cannot be purchased. They cannot be demanded.
They are the fruit of a relationship founded upon gift.
In these days of great effort to bolster human freedom
against the threat of communism we need the constant
reminder spoken by Thomas Jefferson, and enshrined
in his memorial in Washington, that a nation which
forgets that its freedom is a gift from God will not long
endure.

We are called by the name of Christ, and he is in the
midst of us. Here, then, are some of the gifts to us:

Faith Is a Gift

Faith is the gift of response to God, whose care and
renewing love is the manifest nature of history. Indeed,
the self-giving of God in Christ is the center of history.
Every man participates in that central act and thereby
affirms his humanity through encounter and response.
"We know that we have passed out of death and into
life," the early Christians confidently affirmed, "because
we love the brethren." Yet, today, escape from the love

of our brethren into token relations fills all our waking moments. The truth is that we fear and mistrust each other—and where fear is, anger is also.

The result is that the most devastating reality of our lives—yours and mine—is an unrelieved loneliness. Those who suffer loneliness in mental institutions are different from most of us only in degree, not in root cause. They, like many of us, have known fear "in a handful of dust" —in the hazards of human relationships—and as a consequence have withdrawn from the human race. They will be helped, whether by psychotherapy or any other expression of human care, to the extent that they are drawn back into a relationship which makes possible a willingness to risk themselves in encounter. Is this not the balm of Gilead vital for all of us?

Dr. Frieda Fromm-Reichmann, one of our greatest therapists, has done much to demonstrate that even the most seriously disturbed may be recovered when they are drawn back into mutuality. That seems to happen only in the response of faith to the gift of genuine relationship on the part of the therapist. Dr. Fromm-Reichmann tells of working with one patient whose withdrawal had taken the radical form of muteness. For months the doctor worked without response from this patient. Then one day her charge blurted out: "I don't know why you keep trying. I'm not interested!" Negative as they seem, those words encouraged the doctor, and she countered with the suggestion that they proceed on her (that is, the doctor's) faith. A year and a half later, when the patient was really on the road to recovery, she recalled this experience as a turning point in her struggle for health. Here she had come to the conviction that the doctor's interest was a true gift, without conditions. And health returned with faith as a response to that gift.

Hope Is a Gift

We are saved by hope—by the gift of hope which endures all things. There is a shallow thing called "hope," but its tinsel wears off in the first test of experience. Genuine hope runs to *still waters* and *paths of righteousness* even in dark valleys. Why? Because it is the end of history already entering into our lives and lending its completion to our fragmentary existence. It is the shape of that conviction that God has set his love upon us from the beginning. He will not abandon us.

Clinical psychiatry is discovering that children who are made to feel unsure of parental support become adults who live in constant fear of abandonment. They are always wanting to "go home again" only to discover that "home" is a disappointing illusion. But the problem is deeper than clinicians imagine. This is a whole generation of men and women driven by the fear of abandonment. They search a world in which God has been exiled for some word of support and encouragement. Like bewildered children, they seek to find themselves, in one diversion after another. In the end their borrowed identity is forfeited by the impersonality of the formula $E = mc^2$; that is, a world in which all effort is finally reduced to the mere transformation of energy from one impersonal form to another.

There is a word that brings order to this chaos. It is hope, the substance of hope as known in the Bible.

The Lord of creation, who in Jesus Christ reveals himself supremely as the Lord of history, is Lord also because he invests history with hope. His word speaks to our abandonment and becomes in us the hope by which we live between this moment and its fulfillment.

The great enemies of hope in our day are fatalism on the one side and sentimentalism on the other. Both flee from real meeting with Him who knows us in our abandonment and searches us in our false security. Both underestimate our hopelessness apart from the Word of God. But it is precisely here that our hope is born: that God cares and that his Word searches us. This is the hope that has renewed men and nations throughout history.

> Though the fig tree do not blossom,
> Nor fruit be on the vines. . . .
> Yet I will rejoice in the Lord,
> I will joy in the God of my salvation.[4]

Love Is a Gift

One of the saddest commentaries on modern life is what we have done to the word "love" and its other translation, "charity." An effective motto of one of the benevolent organizations is "Not charity but a chance" —and that strikes a responsive chord in every one of us. But place beside that decayed conception of *caritas*, the one held by Paul: "Love (caritas) bears all things, believes all things, hopes all things, endures all things."

Is this the love we know? For many it has become something to be bought—something given only upon cash (or services) rendered. In a marketing world it has even become something like a prize for cheap tricks. One of the advertisements of recent prominence appeals with the slyness and insinuation of the snake in Eden: "Would your husband 'fall' for you today?" The important thing is that these degenerate uses of the word "love" are there because we put them there. Sadly enough, they are expressions of what is true in our own experience. And our experience is the result of all our frantic striving to use love—even love—as a means of manipulation and control of others.

With regard to the gift of love we need the insistent reminder of Christ: "Without me you can do nothing." Nothing! Love is not a reward. It is a free gift. It is from God, who is able when we are impotent. Our virtues will not save us, but love as a free gift is able to save. We cannot take it by violence, nor purchase it, nor demand it. Neither can we generate it from within. But we may have it if we are willing to accept it as a gift. Is not this the depth of love: It is the gift—the unmerited gift—of genuine relationship. This is the secret revealed to children, a veritable bulwark in a grasping world: all is given. Every husband and wife—every parent and child—must learn this lesson if their love is to endure. Faithfulness, the keeping of promises, is built upon the foundation of freely given love. Trust is bestowed. It is response to trustfulness. Mankind has known it in Mary and in those who, like her, are able to receive and to nurture promises. I saw it happen again not long ago when a mother traveling by plane, folded her child to herself and gave him confidence beyond fear or fright.

Freedom Is a Gift

And, like every other gift, it must be shared if it is to be preserved. As Christians we are reminded that our freedom is derived from our faith in Christ. The same thinking which prompted Jefferson to declare that a nation owes its freedom to God, should sustain us when we are assaulted by the bogus claims and half-truths of communism as well as when we are tempted to narrow nationalism. Surely Adlai Stevenson is on solid ground when he reminds us that the great men of America were not great because they achieved "purely American purposes, but because they were able to speak for humanity at large and extend their vision to the whole family of man." The sound of the liberty bell which pealed the joyous note of freedom at this nation's birth is still another reminder of the source of all freedom: "Proclaim liberty throughout the land."

The givenness of that liberty is the solid foundation of our life together. The right text for genuine patriotism is this: "Others have labored, and we have entered into the fruits of their labors." There are more than a hundred thousand American graves on distant shores which represent only a fraction of humanity's tortured bequest to this generation. Shall we betray that trust by turning our back on the extension of freedom which is the challenge of our day? Where fear and suspicion are deliberately manipulated to undermine that trust, freedom is already under grave threat. The great, living, throbbing text which places the challenge of gifts and of gift giving before us as a people is "Stand fast, therefore, in the liberty wherewith Christ hath made us free."

Faith, hope, love, and freedom—these are gifts from God. They appear in the most unexpected ways—in a faraway manger, in a prisoner's cross, and in a child's trust. Certainly these are not the occasions where one expects the power of this world to show itself. Still they are occasions of love—and gift. They are reminders that the weak things of God are stronger than the occasional power of man; for it is the meek, as those emptied of possessions, demands, and knowledge, who are ready to receive gifts and thus to inherit the earth.

• *Notes for Chapter 9*

1. Ephesians 2:8.
2. Ephesians 4:8, referring to Psalm 68:18.
3. John 6:6.
4. Habakkuk 3:17, 18, in part.

10: Person and Family

∾§ . . . of whom the whole family in heaven and earth is named.[1]

IN THORNTON WILDER'S PLAY, "The Skin of Our Teeth," Mrs. Antrobus, near the end, reminds her perennially straying husband of the real basis of their marriage. "I didn't marry you because you were perfect," she tells him. "I didn't even marry you because I loved you. I married you because you gave me a promise." She takes off her wedding band and looks at it. "That promise," she continues, "made up for your faults. And the promise I gave you made up for mine. Two imperfect people got married and it was that promise that made the marriage." Every family consists of "two imperfect people" who have entered into a partnership; and their marriage consists of a promise, not a perfection.

Our identity, whether in our immediate family or in church, rests upon promises—not finished perfections. "What did your sponsors then promise for you?" one is asked concerning his baptism as he prepares to assume mature and confirmed Christian responsibility. "A name and a promise," we are reminded, wherein we were

118

made members of Christ, children of God, and inheritors of the kingdom of Heaven. Our "Christian" name is derived from the occasion when the gift of ourselves was given.

We have been reminding ourselves that our identity is grounded in the intention of God to claim us for his own and to gather us in his love out of the God-forsaken habitations of our own making. The name which we bear is an ever-present reminder that our immediate family is our first church, and that its lasting identity also rests in Him "of whom the whole family in heaven and earth is named." Man is not a weed which "just growed" like Topsy, without care or purpose. He is a creature fashioned in love by One who sets him in a fair land and calls him by name—even in pursuit.

> When Israel was a child, I loved him,
>   and out of Egypt I called my son.
> The more I called them,
>   the more they went from me. . . .[2]

THE FAMILY: THE FIRST CHURCH

The family is the first church. Here we discover our primary identity in the quality of response that greets and calls us unto being. And here it is vitally true that we live by love; or, to put it the other way, that we perish, we die, for lack of love. Paul tells us that "faith comes by hearing." It is equally true that despair comes by hearing. The child is shaped by what he hears, by the reflection of himself encountered in the family and in his immediate world. He hears not so much the words as the melody which accompanies his advent. He lives by love and faith as the immediate, vitally sustaining realities of his life long before he attempts to live by the wisdom and prudence of the world.

What, then, if the only music which the child hears is discord, sound and fury? We have learned a lot about the relation of the family and the child in recent years. The family is the guardian and fashioner of the future person. And this means that those who work with children in trouble must recognize that they are at the same time faced with families in trouble. Healing must come about not merely by restoring an isolated child, but also by helping a whole family to gain a new direction—perhaps, even, a new song. In biblical religion that new song is not a flash "hit," but the music of deep calling unto deep, which turns the hearts of parents to their children and of children to their parents.

It is true that the family has proved itself to be the most adaptable and the most durable of human institutions. Even so, the family is in trouble today. More than one out of every four marriages ends in divorce. And many who do not seek divorce have abandoned all hope or have forgotten their promise. The family is in trouble. Is it, perhaps, because families are presided over by men and women who still want to be children— who flee from their own maturity and waste their years in "riotous" self-pity? Is the deeper cause that we are afraid of response, afraid to be responsible to one another and lacking in that undergirding of love which is able to "bear all things, believe all things, hope all things"? Obviously some honest facing of these questions must take place and, to be sure, apart from pious platitudes which excuse us by being so broad and so innocuous as never to touch any of us. If the family is in trouble that trouble begins *in* and belongs *to* each one of us who have let our own and other families forget who we are. "When a father says, 'I don't know,' isn't that a partial admission that he didn't care?" asks John Steinbeck, the novelist, in a discussion of juvenile delinquency. "And the child who says, 'Hang me,' isn't that a cry that he dies alone?" The juvenile delinquent is a forceful reminder that the world we have made is one in which,

> promises are not kept
> nor one may weep because another wept,

as W. H. Auden put it.

"THE TROUBLE IS IN THEIR LOVING . . ."

One little boy put it this way: "The trouble is in their loving, that's where the trouble is!" He was in a doctor's office and his whole appearance—even his symptoms— were symbolic of the taut, unyielding spirit which prevailed at home. But that little boy placed his finger on more than one family's problem. Lovelessness is the end product of more than one family. It is the destiny of every family where anxious self-centeredness and dishonesty have driven out all that faith and trust could have accomplished.

Add, to this failure of the family to care enough, the fact that we live in a world which teaches its young that anything successful is right, but compensates for its competitiveness *outside* by a demand for tenderness *within*. Here one discovers another virus at the root of the family. For here even "love" becomes a calculated virtue. It is the mask we wear in polite society. Such "love" can neither unite us nor renew us. It is sterile. And the family perishes for want of genuine love. The passion of the midtwentieth century is not love nor freedom, but fear and conformity. Many parents are quite frank to say that they are more concerned that their children be standard products—"regular" boys and girls who will be "accepted" because they fit the pattern. A few years ago a tragic number of these same "adjustable" young men were easily won over by the disciplined "brain washing" of the Communists in North Korea.

It is crucial, therefore, that Christians continually recall their identity in Christ. The New Testament puts it in many metaphors but none more striking than Paul's statement that beyond our fear and bondage we have received the gift of true sonship to God by adoption.[3] Within that spirit we are enabled for freedom—as friends and kinfolk, no longer servants. The adopted son is the "chosen" son—one whose being is affirmed and confirmed by an act of will. And since personal agency is the heart of an act of will, every human family is analogously affirmed or denied in the will, or its lack, in parents. So we return to the fact that gift is the heart of the gospel and our attitude toward that gift is crucial for its acceptance or its rejection in many families. "Love what you are to be," Augustine wrote, "for you will be sons of God and sons of adoption. This will be given you freely and freely conferred upon you."

Every family is identified by the spirit which motivates its members—whether in possessiveness which engenders hate or in sharing which issues in love. The Christian family is promised—not as a hoarded possession, but as a day-by-day gift—not only the power to become sons of God but also the fruits of the spirit, like love, joy, peace. In a loveless world this is possible only within a continual returning and resting in that spirit-community whereby we are enabled for freedom.

Such gifts do not make Christian families immune to the disturbances of family life which beset others. It is only that they may alert us to the new beginnings which are possible after every confessed failure. Is not this the character of a family that knows the strength of a loving father? It is characterized by resiliency and the capacity to work and live in unity even when hope is deferred. Such families are led—not driven—"with cords of compassion, with the bonds of love," as Hosea would say.

HEARING AND BEING HEARD

Some months ago I shared in a workshop of parents and children in the church. The parents were asked to submit their questions. Among them were such queries as "When can I permit my child to make his own decisions?" and "How can I deal with his varying moods?" Then the youngsters were gathered for a panel and asked to complete this statement: *"The trouble with parents is. . . ."* Their composite answer was, "Too bossy and too busy!" I must confess that at that point I felt some identification with Clarence Darrow's remark, namely, that "the first half of our lives is ruined by our parents and the second half by our children"!

It is just possible, however, that we were hearing painful music played back from years in our own families. The person of a child can withstand many shocks, but the parent who "bosses" without being in touch or who takes his or her parental responsibility "on the run" as a barely tolerated interruption can expect children who may conclude that to be an adult is to become a pretender—a "phony"!

Even this kind of shock may prove useful for the Christian family. The beginning of all wisdom is a knowledge of our ignorance. To have *heard* our child, even when truth comes as a sharp-edged sword, is to begin a new relation in touch. Then, perhaps, we may be ready to learn that we can accomplish in repentance what we cannot do in proud self-sufficiency. The real meaning of the Christian family rests in its gifts of love and forbearance of one another. Here the motive is not competition for virtue but a way of saying, "Thanks be to God for setting us in the midst of family and friends."

One heavy pall which hangs over so much of contemporary life is its lack of *hearing*—its inattention. John Ciardi, poet and critic, recently called attention to the fact that one of the seven deadly sins, *acedia,* usually translated *sloth,* is, in fact, the prevailing sin of our day. It is, he says, the failure to pay attention—to give attention—and this is the real meaning of *acedia.*

Now, above all things, a genuine family consists of people who hear one another. The Christian family is centered in Christ, our bond of peace and our only sure ground of mutual hearing. In Christ we are confronted not only with the hardness of our own hearts and our deaf ears but also with a love that wounds our heart and opens our ears. Every time a couple exchange their vows at the altar the church prays "that their home may be a haven of blessing and of peace." It can remain such a haven where members hear one another only as found, not in their habitual hearing of one another, but in Christ. This is the new occasion in Christ—that we hear one another. Hearing is one of the modes of heaven. It is born of God whose "steadfast love" never ceases and yet is "new every morning." The family which abides in such hearing is constant in tribulation and patient in trouble.

For those of you who live with children let me suggest a rewarding exercise. Sometime try entering your child's world as a polite guest—not as an authority. Study his or her play as a most serious occupation in which he is mastering reality and quite incidentally saying something to himself and to you. Let his or her spontaneous language of action be heard.

It may be sobering. It could be revealing. It should be rewarding. You may hear a candid commentary on the limits of your hearing and your participation in your child's world. In any event, a sincere effort to hear another is to come again to the quality of life which marks that family "of whom the whole family in heaven and earth is named."

• *Notes for Chapter 10*

1. Ephesians 3:15 (KJV).
2. Hosea 11:1-2.
3. Romans 8:15,16.

11: If There Be Any Virtue

&8 Finally, brethren, whatsoever things are true, whatsoever
things are honest, whatsoever things are just, whatsoever
things are pure, whatsoever things are lovely, whatsoever things are of good report; if there be any virtue, and
if there be any praise, think on these things.[1]

VIRTUE, according to Socrates, is knowledge of the good.
It is a specific expression of that character and strength
which all men value and some men acquire by discipline. The cardinal virtues according to ancient Greece
were prudence, courage, temperance, and justice. Later,
in Christianity, these were taken over as the natural
virtues, which are dependent upon the supernatural, or
theological, virtues—faith, hope, and love. Together
they constitute the seven virtues that are counter to
the seven deadly sins of medieval fame.

But in the transition from the pagan to the Christian
world the word "virtue" (ἀρετή) has undergone an
interesting transformation. It is used sparingly in the
New Testament—only four times. In the Markean
account of the woman who had been ill for many years
and who touched the hem of Jesus' garment, believing
in its power to heal, the record states, "And Jesus,

immediately knowing in himself that virtue had gone out of him, turned him about in the press, and said, 'Who touched my clothes?' " [2] Again Peter, that early pastor, reminded his flock that it is through the divine power and knowledge of Christ that the Christian is called "to glory and virtue." "Add to your faith, virtue," he wrote; "and to virtue, knowledge." [3]

Now certainly, here, virtue has a close relation to the person and power of Christ. It is a gift of relation rather than a practical accomplishment.

WHEN IS A VIRTUE A VICE?

Perhaps the first Christians saw, as we are unable to see, that virtues easily become vices when they are sought after as individual possessions, apart from the community of faith. Augustine looked upon extracted "virtues" as sources of "inflated pride" by which men forget that it is God who gives the blessed life to men. So the great Bishop of Hippo pointed out to the pagan world that only one who knows the gifts of faith, hope, and love can properly employ the natural virtues without being destroyed by pride from within. And the author of Philippians seems to be saying that *if there be any virtue*, any cause for praise, let it be offered to God as an occasion of thanksgiving.

There is a general impression that to be a Christian is to be a virtuous man or woman. We are scandalized when we experience the opposite. After all, Christ himself said, "By their fruits ye shall know them." But when the fruits become more important than the tree which bears them, it is time to take another look at fundamental relations. Christians who congratulate themselves in a popularized brand of Christianity should take heed of the virtues in which they are exalting. Frequently it turns out that pride has "infiltrated" *them* along with their exalted "virtues"! Their apparent victory has been won, too often, by ignoring the deep chasm that actually exists between "the good that I would" and "the evil that I do"! And the "lies of tongue and pen" as well as "the easy speeches that comfort cruel men" on the lips of the self-righteous sound the note which leads a long procession into hell. It must have been this same phenomenon—this double-mindedness in most men—which prompted T. S. Eliot to pray, "O Lord, deliver me from the man of good intentions and impure heart!"

THE AMBIVALENCE OF MORALISM

A religion which consists solely of moral precepts and calculated virtues is both appealing and dangerous. Its appeal can be measured by the fact that this is the religion of most Christians. It is *the Christianity of Main Street* as Canon Wedel has described it. Almost every day we hear someone extol the Ten Commandments and the Golden Rule as their "religion." This is all very well if one keeps in mind that "right" action is rooted in a single heart. Otherwise the judgment contained in these statements is obscured in an effort to reduce the gospel to a set of rules. It is comforting to have such neat summaries of such earth-shaking realities. Comforting—but also dangerous because it obscures the Cross in every command—even in the

Golden Rule—and it lures its advocate into believing that he can discover the strength of life in rules rather than in personal commitment. But the heart is not in such a religion. At best it is only a halfway commitment.

In a world where brutal ideologies are struggling for absolute ascendancy over the soul of man, such a double-minded religion will easily fall. The Communists are right when they proclaim that a religion of middle-class virtues will not stand before their single-minded zeal. But they will meet their match in the Christian for whom the moral life and its virtues are crowns cast before the throne of Almighty God in thankful adoration. True virtue comes from the strength of being which is grounded in God alone: " 'Not by might, nor by power, but by my Spirit,' says the Lord of Hosts." [4]

It is characteristic of moralism to be primarily concerned with "What ought I to do?" rather than with "Who is Lord?" It is concerned with conduct rather than person, with results rather than responses. It is easy, then, to assume that the demands of the moral life are fulfilled when one is correct, but without responsibility—and that the drive behind action is consistency rather than loyalty. Paul revealed the ambivalence behind all moralism when he declared, "If I speak with the tongues of men and of angels and have not love, I am sounding brass and tinkling cymbal."

Let us admit it! A lot of our so-called virtues are "sounding brass." In an ethos where the prevailing morality is dictated by what is expected and high premiums are paid for conformity, "virtue" is apt to be used as a mask which hides an anxious, pride-consumed heart turned in upon itself. Meanwhile the person is robbed

of his true identity—symbolized in his Christian name—
as more and more he becomes an anonymous host to a
world of claims. Pirandello has pictured this phenomenon in his play, "As You Desire Me." And one person
victimized by this demon said: "I'm just a collection of
mirrors reflecting what everyone else expects of me!"

One of the prevailing dissemblances of our day is
the use of virtuous slogans to cover our cowardice and
insensitiveness. Our first concern in every question
seems to be not "What is true?" but "What is safe?"
Virtue comes to be embodied in such slogans as "He
does not make trouble," "He never gets out of line."
Hence, as Camus puts it in his novel, *The Fall*, "Mod-
esty helped me to shine, humility to conquer, and virtue
to oppress."

In each case virtue has become a tool by which one
manipulates others or is himself manipulated. In either,
the person is more alone, more defeated as a result of
this spurious use of virtues. How many families suffer
a fracture of their relationships because essentially both
parents and children are more absorbed in being right
than in being in touch—and each expects the other to
justify his claim of perfection. Do you remember Willie
Loman in *The Death of a Salesman?* He had become a
commodity—a thing to be used. He also had two rules.
The first was "Always get there first, ahead of the
other man." The second rule was "Always be well
liked." Near the end, after his discharge, he kept saying
to himself in bewilderment, "But I was the best liked!"

VIRTUE AND VIRTUES IN THE
CHRISTIAN COMMUNITY

The proper relation between virtue and virtues, between faith and works, may perhaps be seen in the New Testament view of the relation between *being* and *doing*. In one of the passages of the Sermon on the Mount, Christ warns his disciples that not everyone who calls after him, "Lord, Lord," but he who does the Lord's work, will enter the Kingdom. Then he turns around and warns those who claim great works accomplished in his name, "Depart from me . . . for I never knew you." Man is man not simply by *doing;* he must also *be*. Doing and being belong together in the Christian view. The warning is clear: works—even good works—apart from the motivations of response to God become as nothing.

But you may object that even so the gospel lays heavy claims upon the Christian: "Except your righteousness exceeds the righteousness of the Scribes and Pharisees. . . ." The imperatives are there, but it is important to remember that they are meant for and laid upon those who have known the prior love of God in Christ. Apart from the forgiving love manifest in Christ, every command, every rule, every "ought," becomes a heavy burden, "grievous to be bourne." The Christian life of response to these imperatives is posited upon the gift of grace in Christ. The Reformers said that man always tends to remember only the second table of the Decalogue—without the first. He is struck by the claims of God but forgets, as Augustine had put it, that God commands what he gives and gives what he commands. The essence of the gospel is grace, not law.

Here, then, is the urgent relevance of the church and of sacramental action to our moral life. If there be any virtue in the Christian community, it is an occasion for thanksgiving for the experienced victory over death in the midst of life. The significance of Christ in the church is the fact that a new life is already present here. It is the kingdom of God *beginning to come.* Virtue in such a community is its wider sacramental action in which all of God's creation is beginning to be claimed as sacred in the light of what is manifest. Here "we are very members incorporate in the mystical body of Christ," as the Prayer Book puts it, and He is incarnate in us as "the blessed company of all faithful people." Virtue and community become one in the sacramental existence of Jesus Christ.

Within the church the motive for sacramental action is not an alien, outside compulsion but response to kinship at the heart of existence. As Paul puts it in Galatians, "In Christ Jesus you are all sons of God through faith . . . and because you are sons, God has sent the spirit of his Son into our hearts, crying Abba! Father!" [5] Such a relationship is grounded in the uniquely personal sharing of deep calling unto deep— it is *to-be-found-of-God* in the depths and, in that *being-found,* to discover that God hears with infinite love.

Bishop Brent used to say that "simplicity is not doing one thing; it is doing all things from one motive." In the church this single-hearted motivation is provided through the structure of a family life and a congregational life which knows itself to be the living Body of Christ. In this renewing life we are transfigured as we behold and live into the image of Christ: by means of baptism and daily dying unto ourselves, by means of repentance and confession as speaking the truth in love, by means of forgiveness and daily Eucharist, thereby appropriating the event of Christ in faith.

Our virtue as Christians is our daily renewal in communion with one another in Christ where as we behold his glory we are made in his image—and creation is restored to its expectancy, that is, waiting for the harvest of God's planting. To be a person in the deepest sense is to be identified with such virtue, to bear its eternity in our time, to participate in its reality, and to taste its fruit. It is ours when we offer ourselves, our souls and bodies, in thanksgiving. For the hallowing of God's gifts is the end and purpose of every virtue.

• *Notes for Chapter 11*

1. Philippians 4:8 (KJV).
2. Mark 5:30 (KJV).
3. II Peter 1:3,5 (KJV).
4. Zechariah 4:6.
5. Galatians 3:26 and 4:6.

12: How Does God Make Us Free?

⤸ Now the Lord is the Spirit, and where the Spirit of the Lord is, there is freedom. And we all, with unveiled face, beholding the glory of the Lord, are being changed into his likeness from one degree of glory to another; for this comes from the Lord who is the Spirit.[1]

YOU MAY RECALL Paul's statement in Galatians 5 which, like his hymn to love in I Corinthians 13, comes nearer than any other to a setting forth of the Christian virtues. But they are not virtues in the ordinary sense because they are the "fruit" of a relationship rather than goals of perfection. And like fruit they cannot be produced apart from the living organism which bears them. In Galatians, Paul was writing a letter to his former flock, some of whom, he had learned, were doing strange things in order to make doubly sure that their salvation was secure. They were insisting on all the old requirements of the Hebrew ritual law within the Christian community. They were turning back to the burdensome tyranny of the law.

The Apostle viewed this action with alarm. It meant to him that their self-centered anxiety had not really been replaced by a faith-trust relation to the free gift

134

of God's grace in Jesus Christ. Their action struck at the roots of the new covenant "not in a written code but in the spirit." "If we live by the Spirit," Paul reminds them, "let us also walk by the Spirit!" In the preceding passage he had put the relation of faith and works in the proper order: " . . . the fruit of the Spirit is love, joy, peace, patience, kindness, goodness, faithfulness, gentleness, self-control; against such there is no law." [2] This momentous defense of the freedom of the spirit and of the proper relation between faith and works has been the heart of every great renewal in Christian history whether of Augustine, the Reformers, John Wesley, or of modern man's groping effort to rediscover the vitality of his faith. And these fruits of the Spirit have been springs of refreshment in the desert of man's history since Paul.

Still, it is important that we appreciate what a radical difference this understanding of the good life is in contrast to the ordinary "do's and don'ts" of polite society. It is man's declaration of freedom from meticulous casuistry and petty moralism. For Paul it opened man for freedom, for a life sustained by grace beyond law; and it was the solid foundation behind Augustine's exclamation: "Love God and do what you will."

FREEDOM AND LORDSHIP

It is in this understanding, then, that Paul addresses another congregation: "Now the Lord is the Spirit, and where the Spirit of the Lord is, there is freedom." [3] The Greek word for Lord here is *Kurios*—the same word which was used in reference to the Emperor. Paul employs it some 250 times in references to Jesus Christ, the one Lord. Professor Hort, one of the greatest New Testament scholars, suggests that a slight change be made in the second part of our text from *Kuriou* to *Kurion* and it thus becomes, "Where the Spirit is Lord, there is liberty." [3] In this light, Jesus' words to Nicodemus take on added significance. The Spirit, like the wind, blows where it will. One may hear the sound of it but cannot tell "whence it comes or whither it goes." It is not subject to man's control. It can neither be found locally nor be possessed individually. But wherever the Spirit is Lord there also is freedom. Indeed, freedom then is the mode of man's response to the Lordship of the Spirit. It is the means whereby man as man finds himself, becomes himself, fulfills himself under God. (We hardly need to add that freedom is always accompanied by the creative pains of new birth.)

Lewis Sherrill has written that "the theme of Lordship [in the Bible] is pointed toward the predicament of man's freedom." In other words, the Lordship of God is the other side of man's freedom. Only within that relationship is man free. Rootless freedom is always an illusion. In a reversal of Lewis Sherrill's terms, it (that is, rootless freedom) *is pointed toward the predicament of man's slavery.* The tyranny of impulse, as any man who has taken a hand to direct himself will tell you, is not overcome by setting oneself adrift in a sea of expediency. It must be met by commitments whose anchorage will not be dragging in every storm. In the Book of Common Prayer one is reminded of this truth week by week as prayers are addressed to God, "the author of peace and lover of concord . . . whose service is perfect freedom." Freedom belongs to commitment and service.

BUT HOW?

Even so, you may ask, How do we get from where we are, all bogged down as we are with daily "oughts" and with the bitter fruits of our own little religion? How do we get from this barricaded, hemmed-in existence to the glorious liberty of the children of God? We can describe the Christian life, but how does it become effective in our life? We, like Moses, are always standing just outside the promised land. Now and then we catch a glimpse of its beauty and are touched by its passion. But we know that we shall not pass over into it. The question that haunts our soul is not *what* the good life is but *how* it is entered. We can suffer fools more gladly than preachers who keep on telling us what religion means but never *how!*

Interestingly enough, the same question in a slightly different form was asked by John Ciardi, poet and critic, in an article entitled, "The Way to a Poem" in *The Saturday Review* some months ago. He emphasized that the proper question is not *what* a poem means but *how* it means. He illustrated by using a favorite from Robert Frost, "On Stopping by Woods on a Snowy Evening." Do you recall?

> Whose woods these are I think I know.
> His house is in the village though;
> He will not see me stopping here
> To watch his woods fill up with snow.

My little horse must think it queer
To stop without a farmhouse near
Between the woods and frozen lake
The darkest evening of the year.
He gives his harness bells a shake
To ask if there is some mistake.
The only other sounds the sweep
Of easy wind and downy flake.
The woods are lovely, dark and deep,
But I have promises to keep,
And miles to go before I sleep
And miles to go before I sleep.[4]

The poem does not talk *about* meaning; it *is* meaning. It is as Robert Frost himself has said " . . . a momentary stay against confusion. . . . It is an arrest of disorder." One is reminded of Robert Browning's sentiment,

God is the perfect poet,
Who in his person
Acts his own creations.[5]

Poetry draws one into an experience touched with emotion and meaning that cannot be communicated apart from the living enactment which it is. Dorothy Sayers has said much the same thing in response to the question, "What do you mean by this book?" "The book itself is what the writer means," she answers. The meaning is not somehow separate and apart from the work of the artist. It is a wedding of craftsmanship and creative purpose. Perhaps there is something of this wedding preserved in the word "poet." In the old Scot's tongue the poet is "the maker"; he shares some of the creativeness of the Maker of all things. Now in much the same way God "means" in our life. Emil Brunner has written, "It is genuine communication which remains bound to the act of communication." [6] The way of God's meaning in our lives remains bound to the actions of God in Christ and in history in which we encounter both his judgment and his grace. We are persons after the mode of heaven. Our identity is centered in the identity of God which we know not in a vacuum but in the modes, the actions, the events through which he is revealed to ourselves! God's way of making us over in faith and in meaning are conveyed in the modes of his revelation, which becomes ours in faithful participation. Perhaps this is the reason why the theologians constantly remind us that the content of revelation is not some "thing" but God himself.

Speaking of theology, we are reminded that its proper function is the clarification and critical evaluation of religious faith and practice. Theological students need the constant reminder that the inevitable abstractions of theology can never take the place of the living commitment and participation which is the prior reality of faith. Not many of us will spend our lives as technical theologians seeking to answer the question, "*What* is the meaning of Christianity?" That is an important task, but it must be carried forward by those who can take their place in the great conversation with philosophy and science. But every Christian who in faith and trust has laid his gift upon the altar, whether of pain or joy, and has gone forth charged with new strength of grace, knows *how* Christianity means.

ON BEING CHANGED IN HIS LIKENESS

Within the church, where the Spirit is Lord, freedom is the mark of the person. The free person is not compelled to live either by "positive thinking" or Stoic effort. He lives by entering into a common life whose being and becoming is grounded in God—the same God who has set his love upon man from eternity. The heartbeat of this community is returning and rest, quietness and confidence, knowing and being known, forgiveness and forgiving—a life "in all places of His dominion" which has been caught up in praise and thanksgiving.

> Praise the Lord, O my soul, and all that is within me,
> Praise his holy name.[7]

Such a life commends itself to us not by its superior philosophy, nor even by its sterling virtues, but by its devotion and its transfiguring witness. The church is the first fruit of God's promise in the gospel. Its life rests entirely upon God's way of making. We are able to discern some of these dimensions.

First, the Lordship of God is expressed in his making, fashioning, judging, and redeeming activity. From the beginning of the biblical account, God not only creates man and breathes life into him but he also shapes and fashions man in his own image. Paul reminds his congregations again and again that Lordship is crucial in the fashioning process. "You belong to the power which you choose to obey," he declares. Again he reminds them that through baptism which was their own choice they now belong to Christ whose unfathomable gift is eternal life. Yet the gift is given in the manner of this earth. Christ is always challenging the doubting Thomas in us: "Handle me and see!"

Second, the response to that gift is better entered into and enjoyed than explained. God's action means in such a way that we appropriate it for ourselves as we enter a poem, or sing a hymn, or join a procession. It is a genuinely *new* experience. A. D. Lindsay has said that the saints are not people who merely *do* more than ordinary people. "Gracious conduct is something like the work of an artist," he writes. "It needs imagination and spontaneity . . . the creation of something new." Jesus compared God's action to a man who prepared a great feast and bade his guests to come. His love is a bidding love: "Come, for all things are ready!" We who are invited can either enter into the festival joy of our host, or hold back with a raft of shaky excuses. But, accepted or not, the invitation stands—for all men, at all times, in all places. Our God is not a capricious host.

Third, to accept the invitation is to know and to enter into the meaning of obedience—in faith. This is the heart of the gospel. The primary meaning of obedience is to hear at the deepest level. By contrast we tend to make of obedience a compulsion by some alien force. But obedience in its original sense rests upon a personal relation and free choice, whether in Abraham in primitive absolute trust offering his son, or Christ who, in obedience to his mission, humbled himself upon the cross. Indeed, one might well define the biblical view of man as the creature who in personal obedience can make and keep promises. The sacraments are the prototypes of Christian obedience and therefore of Christian moral action. They are thoroughly centered in the biblical mode of revelation. They invite participation rather than individual heroics. They recall us to our first humanity as well as to our first identity through action and faith. They restore us to the vision of the whole; for we being many are made one in Christ.

Christianity is more than an idea; it is to be caught up in a round of life which is an extension of those sacred acts by which God in Christ has touched our life with truth and eternity. It is to be made perfect in every good work because it is God himself who works within us. It is to be transfigured as we behold his image, take upon ourselves his yoke and enter into the fullness of his joy. " 'Then what must we do,' they asked him, 'if we are to work as God would have us work?' Jesus replied, 'This is the work that God requires: believe in the one whom he sent.' " [8]

This is how the Lord makes us free!

• *Notes for Chapter 12*

1. II Corinthians 3:17-18.

2. Galatians 5:25,22,23.

3. Hence, J. K. Mozley in his commentary on II Corinthians in Gore's one-volume commentary, page 521, states: "In that case Hort's minute emendation of Kuriou into Kurion at the end of [verse] 17 has much in its favor and we should translate, 'Where the Spirit is Lord.' "

4. *The Complete Poems of Robert Frost.* Copyright 1923 by Holt, Rinehart and Winston, Inc. Reprinted by permission of Holt, Rinehart and Winston, Inc.

5. Paracelsus, Part II.

6. H. Emil Brunner, *Revelation and Reason* (Philadelphia: The Westminster Press, 1946), p. 370.

7. Psalm 103:1 (BCP).

8. John 6:28,29 (NEB, New English Bible).

PART FOUR ⁊

Transfiguring Grace

Grace is the gift of Christ, who exposes the gulf which separates God and Man, and, by exposing it, bridges it.

Karl Barth [1]

"She is the manifest measurement of God's glory correcting time."

Charles Williams [2]

---

[1] In *The Epistle to the Romans* (New York: Oxford University Press, 1933).

[2] Joseph, of Mary, in the play "Grab and Grace," *Seed of Adam, and Other Plays* (London: Oxford University Press, 1948).

13: This Holy Discontent

≈§ O, might those sighs and tears return again
Into my breast and eyes, which I have spent,
Mourn with some fruit, as I have mourned in vain.[1]

"WE GATHER OUR ARMS full of guilt as though it were precious stuff," John Steinbeck has written. And he adds, "It must be that we want it that way." There is profound truth in this observation. Guilt is both a burden to man and the concomitant of his desired freedom. To be human is to risk oneself in human relationship—to risk the burden of responsibility and guilt. The resistance as well as the response of the other is necessary for the emergence of the person. To be sure, man wants it that way! The risk of guilt and the possibility of forgiveness are unavoidable alternatives in claiming one's freedom.

The deeper burden in man's soul is unresolved guilt. It is the erosion that finally undermines all hope. It is the unspoken barrier between those who, although they live in proximity to one another, have never discovered the mutuality of love beyond fear and distrust. Guilt, unresolved, feeds upon itself. It is to be without hope and without the expectation of turning,

> Because I do not hope to turn again
> Because I do not hope
> Because I do not hope to turn.

These words from T. S. Eliot's "Ash Wednesday Meditation" portray the dilemma of modern man as he approaches a season of penitence. If he does not hope to turn, if he refuses to recognize his guilt, the burden of guilt remains without the fruit of hope.

Despite himself, however, contemporary man is rediscovering the reality of guilt. The psychiatrists have learned empirically that man suffers guilt. As psychiatrists, however, they appear to be more concerned to find an explanation for guilt than to hear it as the voice of a bona fide conscience. The physicists too have experienced the shock of guilt in recent history but, like most of us, they are bewildered by the task of fitting it into a contemporary world view. The ordinary man would like to deny or ignore guilt but, in that, he is like the patient in Kierkegaard's parable who denies that he has a fever. The signs are unmistakable and open to observation by all. Where life and the breath of hope remain, the symptoms of guilt appear also—even when they are denied. The resolution of guilt begins *only* when its reality is an accepted fact.

GUILT AS A PHENOMENON

Many psychiatrists are taking the reality of guilt more seriously these days. Among them are the existen-

tial analysts who represent a new dimension in psychiatry.[2] They hold that man experiences guilt in three
areas, described by the use of German expressions:

First, there is *Eigenwelt,* one's own world. Here guilt
is experienced as the challenge of creativity. The fact
that man is a self-conscious creature who knows guilt
also implies self-transcendence: namely, the capacity
to remember the past and to imagine the future while
acting in the present moment. But creativity is also an
embarrassment to man and an occasion of his fall. The
fact that man flees from this creativity and prefers to
bury his talent rather than risk it in commitment means
that he suffers guilt. Like the anxious one-talent man of
the parable, he loses even that which he had!

Second, we experience guilt in relation to others who
make up our *Mitwelt.* Every human relationship bears
the possibility of mutual destruction as well as of
mutual love. In one degree or another we are all the
sons of Cain who destroy our brothers by neglect or
jealousy as well as by violence. But murder, whatever
its weapon, leaves its evidence of indelible stain.

Third, and finally, we are alienated from the world
of nature, our *Umwelt.* And guilt for this lost relation is
a deep motif in contemporary life. Perhaps this is one
of the reasons why our recreation is so flat and unsatis-
fying. It is not re-creating because too often our contact with nature becomes, instead of an occasion for
the recovery of our relation to the whole, another
opportunity to exploit creation for our own purposes.
A sunset or a waterfall is lost forever to those whose
only measure of the sun and the water is the depth of
their sun tan! The analysts describe guilt where they

encounter it; that is, as a phenomenon of existence. They are not concerned, as was the psalmist,[3] that man's sin is ultimately before God.

GUILT BEFORE GOD?

In another place, Steinbeck writes that "men seem to be born with a debt they can never repay no matter how hard they try." The weight of this debt becomes more burdensome in a world which does not recognize its deepest source—and has, unwittingly, removed its only means of absolving. In that famous parable of the madman, Nietzsche declares exultantly, "God is dead. God remains dead. And we have killed him." But when the announcement strikes no cord of recognition, his madman acknowledges reluctantly that he has come too early, his time is not yet. "This tremendous event is still on its way . . . ," he explains. "It has not yet reached the ears of man . . . *and yet they have done it themselves.*"[4] The shattering reality that he lives in a world which is without God has not yet reached the ears of most men. They live with the consequences without recognizing the fact. Where God is dead, man becomes a nomad without a home on earth, a heaven above, or a future to look to—all life becomes indifferent, and man is a sojourner without a place to go. Modern literature from Dostoyevsky to William Faulkner seems to be preoccupied with man's homelessness and his consequent anger and guilt. Like Job, man has drunk of "the wrath of the Almighty" and having known *only* this bitterness, the taste lingers on in undisciplined anger and unresolved guilt.

Some people approach the problem of finding a remedy for guilt in much the same manner that a householder visits the hardware store: in other words, hoping to find in the varied assortment just the right gadget to fix it—at a bargain rate! But guilt does not yield to cheap remedies. It seeps back into our lives like an offending odor. Those who purchase "peace of mind" at bargain rates, whether of alcohol or of religion, are apt to feel cheated—without knowing quite why.

In contrast to the contemporary mood you will find surprisingly little about "guilt" in the Bible. The writers did not speculate or compose learned tracts about sin either. They simply reckoned with it as reality. They did not have to remind themselves, as an Army sergeant used to remind me when military routines bogged down with exasperating regularity, "Chaplain," he would say calmingly, "human nature is so prevalent." The writer of II Esdras perhaps, put it more poetically:

> O Adam, what have you done?
> For though it was you who sinned,
> The fall was not yours alone,
> But ours also who are your descendants.
> For what good is it to us,
> If an eternal age has been promised to us,
> But we have done the deeds which bring death?[5]

THE WORK OF GUILT: HOLY DISCONTENT

Man knows guilt as a wracking of his conscience. It is the substance of his life apart from grace. It is inward *dis-grace;* it is wrath and the tyranny of "ought." Guilt is always an invitation to self-pity. Kierkegaard, the great Danish theologian, said that man "clutches his torment because it gives him a right to be resentful. . . ." It does not occur to him that the trouble may lie *within himself*. So the guilty man hauls the whole world into court—including God—and counters his own guilt by charges of injustice. This is the case with Job who was so "put-out" because the Lord never gave him a bill of particulars.

We are a people who know guilt and, consequently, a people who know wrath. Our chief preoccupation seems to be one of either writing or reading books in which we not only *look back in anger*, but tend to see all things in terms of the promises which we or someone else have not kept. Guilt turns every promise into a reproach. No wonder the Israelites killed the prophets and stoned those who were sent unto them. They were a people responding in a quite normal fashion to the conscience-disturbing truth that, for all their light-hearted assumption of obligation at Sinai— "All that Thou hast commanded we will do and be obedient" —for all that, they were guilty not only of disobedience but also of murderous pride. "Better to languish in hell than to be a servant in heaven"; this is Satan's continuing justification for his contemptuous pride in the face of his exposed guilt.

The truth is that guilt cannot be faced as *our* guilt for the same reason that wrath cannot be faced as God's wrath, until we see both in the light of grace. John Donne is right. The pain of guilt is to have mourned in vain. Our guilt becomes a "holy discontent" only when the same grace that reveals our distance from God in his wrath *also* closes that distance in love. Thus the

God who lends us life also lends us a heart of thankful-
ness—even in the shadow of a wasted life or of a painful departure. Father Mapple met the moment of death
with this prayer on his lips:

> "O Father! Chiefly known to me by Thy rod, mortal and
> immortal, here I die. I have striven to be Thine, more
> than this world's, or mine own. Yet this is nothing: I
> leave eternity to Thee; for what is man that he should
> live out the time of his God?" [6]

Here it is important to remember that the absolute
claims which are laid upon man in the New Testament
are meant for those who know the prior love of God.
Apart from that love these claims can be experienced
only as wrath and burden. Every claim of Christ upon
our lives must be prefaced with the reminder that as
Paul puts it, He was made to be sin for our sake. The
same apostle writes that Christ took our bondage in
sin with all its legal demands and set them aside, "nail-
ing them to the Cross." In the wake of that love we are
to let guilt be a means of recovering our lost relation
to God. A wise doctor of my acquaintance leads his
patients to the understanding that illness is a reminder
of the purpose of life. It is an enforced pause for
recollection. Guilt is a reminder also; it is a recollection
of our identity and of the promises we have to keep.
   Indeed, the capacity to experience guilt is of the
very nature of man's humanity. It is *sui generis*. Nietzsche held that "man is the animal that can make promises." This being true, man is also the creature who
knows what it is to break promises. His conscience is
the mark of his transcendence. Paul pays man the

compliment of calling him "inexcusable," that is, he is not merely a passive recipient of action but a responsible initiator—and therefore guilty. He not only "feels" guilt. He *is* guilty! A psychiatry which reduces all guilt to "reaction formation" is not only failing to see the whole phenomenon of man but it is also undermining the very freedom and *self-transcendence* which makes it possible for man to make creative use of psychiatric insight!

HEARTY REPENTANCE AND TRUE FAITH

There are at least three ways of handling guilt:

• One may deny it and repress it, in which case it becomes a tumor gradually strangling every living nerve of one's spiritual life. Surely all of us know those who keep digging at themselves and their world in a futile effort to bury guilt. Unresolved guilt lives on in the harried, self-righteous bore—inside and outside the church. The effort to ignore guilt has a way of becoming the "worst-kept secret" in any person's life.

• Another way of handling guilt is by means of expiation, either in rituals which require elaborate and continuous refinement, as in legalism, or in the manifold obsessions that revolve around the various themes of neurosis. It has been said with some justice that whereas the Catholic in confession and penance buries his sins, the Protestant gives them a prolonged funeral. In either case, Freud was right in his warning that nature does not deal gently with a troubled conscience buried in a shallow grave or walled over with anxious expedients.

• Guilt is adequately handled only when one is able to face it in "hearty repentance and true faith." Whether in psychiatry or in religion one is enabled to face up to his own responsibility only when the strength of his trust is equal to the task of turning away from his old ways and toward new ways.

Between man's guilt and his repentance, God has set the passion of our Lord Jesus Christ. In the picturesque language of Luther, God clothes us in the body of Christ, exchanging it for the thick hide inherited from Adam. We are wrapped and swaddled in Christ. As John Bright has put it in one of our loveliest hymns,

> Look, Father, look on His anointed face,
> And only look on us as found in Him.

To be found in Christ is to find the means of our true identity—beyond the anger and guilt which are the bitter fruit of a dehumanized rootless world. The review title of a recent psychological book proclaimed with unconscious irony its theme: "Survival in a world of probable objects"! But man is more than an "object" and to live is more than "survival." God flung back the challenge of that hopelessness in tidings of great joy proclaimed from a lowly stable in the Palestinian countryside some two thousand years ago.

Repentance is *first* to see ourselves as found in Christ —as found in his for-give-ness and grace. *Second*, it is a turning to one another in reconciliation in the light of that grace. And *finally*, it is to offer ourselves, our souls and bodies thanksgivingly in response to God's gift. Repentance, then, is the true imitation of Christ. It is to claim ourselves—guilt and all—response-ably under grace. There can be no doubt that the confession of guilt and the miracle of forgiveness make up the revolutionary heart of Christianity. They are the bread and wine which seals every human being as a priest who offers the sacrament of new life to his brother for Christ's sake. In the Eastern Orthodox churches the feast of Easter is preceded by a literal enactment of the words of Christ: every member of a family asks and receives the forgiveness of every other member before making his own Eucharist at the altar of the Risen Lord.

Repentance—*metanonia*—is revolutionary also in the sense that it attributes freedom and the capacity for reorientating life to the very core of man's being. Repentance is the other side of man's capacity to experience guilt. It is the *Magna Carta* of our spiritual liberty.

FORGIVENESS AS A WAY OF KNOWING

Man does not come to forgiveness short of a broken spirit and a contrite heart; but even these must be offered sacrificially. Else repentance falls short of forgiveness. "In the sacred history of man on earth," Ignazio Silone says through one of his characters, "it is still, alas, Good Friday." If repentance is a passionate intention to view all things after the mode of heaven, forgiveness is a way of knowing in love. Such knowledge requires sacrifice—not the sacrifice of the zealot proving his worth, but of the recipient of love responding in kind. It has been suggested that the most propitious setting for the beatitudes is to hear them as if from the Cross. Here our hearing of the words is accompanied by our response to the figure on the Cross; and the sacrificial cost, as well as His love, is inescapable.

We are reminded that the one condition set upon our receiving forgiveness in the Lord's Prayer is our own forgiveness of others; forgiveness is the bedrock foundation of any community including the family. But it is to be remembered that "forbearing one another in love" is not a natural virtue. Try it sometime apart from the gifts of faith, hope, and love which are ours under God. Hate is love frustrated by its own incapacity to create itself. Indeed, self-destruction may be viewed as a final commentary upon love which has not been rescued from its own loneliness. Forgiveness is a form of love, and love is in-between. Love is not love until it finds love in-between. Rilke put it with the poet's sensitive touch,

> What will you do, God, when I die
> When I, your vessel, broken lie.
> I am your work; the trade you ply—
> What will you do, God, when I die? [7]

In guilt, repentance, and forgiveness we are changed, not so much by trying harder but by looking closer at ourselves as found in Christ. Guilt, then, is this holy discontent which we all know and which may be turned to fruit only by looking through the eye of grace. It becomes the occasion when we know ourselves forgiven and thereby are enabled to know all things in love.

• *Notes for Chapter 13*

1. John Donne, "Holy Sonnets," *The Penguin Book of Sonnets* (New York: Penguin Books, 1943), p. 164.

2. See Rollo May *et al.*, *Existence: A New Dimension in Psychiatry and Psychology* (New York: Basic Books, 1958).

3. Psalm 51:4.

4. *Existentialism from Dostoyevsky to Sartre*, Walter Kaufman, ed. (New York: Meridian Books, 1956), pp. 105-106.

5. II Esdras 7:45-49.

6. Herman Melville, *Moby Dick* (New York: Harper & Brothers).

7. Rainer Maria Rilke, in *Poems from the Book of Hours*, Babette Deutsch, tr. Copyright 1941 by New Directions. Reprinted by permission of New Directions, Publishers.

14: Begin Now

≈§ If we live by the Spirit, let us also walk by the Spirit.[1]

. . . Behold, now is the acceptable time; behold, now is the day of salvation.[2]

JUST OUTSIDE a small American town there is a cemetery which like many of its kind boasts of "perpetual care." Nearby, a bulldozer which has just demolished one hill looks hungrily across the road and waits its time. The dikes which we build against the flood of time are better tokens of our anxiety than effective means of holding back the future and its change. Time does not respect our promises of "perpetual care." Instead, it bears rootless men and women who have wasted their years in an anxious search for perpetuity, back to the same anonymous, impartial earth.

Our attitude toward time is indicative of our inner divisions which keep us forever without commitment and without identity. We like to think of ourselves as "time savers"; yet there is hardly one of us who does not have trouble with deadlines and commitments. Even in this day of packaged parts and simple directions for

157

"doing it yourself" we are apt to find it difficult to get started, particularly where the start involves a commitment of ourselves. In this we are kin to that old sailor in A. A. Milne's poem,

> There was once an old sailor my grandfather knew,
> Who had so many things he wanted to do,
> That whenever he thought it was time to begin
> He couldn't because of the state he was in!

One of the greatest preachers of the nineteenth century, Frederick W. Robertson, observed that people have the same hesitancy of committing themselves to the Christian life. Instead they say: " 'If I could be sure what is truth, then I would set to work to live in earnest.' " "No," Robertson insisted, "God says act . . . live in earnest and you will know the answer to what is truth."

THE TRUTH THAT MUST ALWAYS BE LEARNED ANEW

Here, then is the message of our combined texts: "Begin now to walk in the Spirit." There are few of us who would be particularly challenged if this admonition involved merely a willingness to stand up and be counted as Christians. That is far too easy. The real test would come if we were suddenly to understand that this word is a radical "either/or," calling into question our actual religion which is in sharp contrast to our easy professions. The call to "begin now" comes as judgment upon many of us who profess to live by the Spirit but who actually walk day by day under every

other spirit except one of obedience and trust in Jesus
Christ. For example, test yourself by comparison to this
description of early Christians walking in the Spirit:

> ... in all things approving ourselves as the ministers of
> God, in much patience, in afflictions, in necessities, in
> distresses ... as sorrowful, yet always rejoicing; as poor,
> yet making many rich; as having nothing, and yet pos-
> sessing all things.[3]

No wonder Peter, the great pastor of the early church,
could write to his flock and remind them that through
their "confidence" which stemmed from their faith and
hope in God, obedience should have become "native"
to them.[4]

But obedience is not "native" to most of us, and the
whole question of appropriation of God's gifts hinges
upon our coming to know something of the infinite difference and yet kinship between God and ourselves,
between God's time and our time. It was this incisive
knowledge that gave biblical religion a common motif:
"The fear of the Lord is the beginning of wisdom." The
scandal of Christianity is that this truth must be learned
anew in every moment. Who is *not* disturbed by the
fact that God is always appearing on the neatly arranged thresholds of our lives and demanding a radi-
cally new dimension in our commitment. "Begin now,"
he insists in Christ, "to walk in the Spirit."

BEGIN NOW TO WALK IN THE SPIRIT

There are three little words here which may help to
make the meaning clearer by a deeper understanding.

The first is the word *now*. The New Testament is full of this word and others close to it which point up the significance of the deciding moment. Hence, Simeon, the man of God who had waited long and devoutly for the Messiah, broke into a hymn of praise when the Christ child was brought into his presence. "Lord, *now* lettest thou thy servant depart in peace," he chanted; and history has taken up the refrain, "for mine eyes have seen thy salvation." Again, Christ startled the woman at the well who had asked an essentially snobbish question which revealed her dilettante heart, with words full of judgment, "The hour cometh and *now* is when the true worshipers shall worship the Father in spirit and in truth." Again, the Johannine writer assures his brothers in the faith, many of whom had already seen the portents of persecution ahead, that their identity in Christ is imperishable, "*Now*, brothers, we are the sons of God."

In each case this word "now" poses the question of whether we have really understood the radical difference which biblical history and Christ make for our understanding of time. For most of us the calendar with its succession of squares for the days of the month is a symbol of the meaning of time. This is measured time, linear time, *chronos* time. It may be surprising, then, to hear that the Hebrew had no equivalent word. The nearest approach to *chronos* time for the Hebrew occurred in phrases like "in the year that King Uzziah died. . . ." It is the significance of time, not its measurement, that is uppermost for the Hebrew. Most important is the fact that for all biblical religion, time belongs to God. In the fullness of time God reveals him-

self to man in and through the events of history. This is
Kairos time, crisis time, packed with significance for
man's deciding. So Paul in our Corinthian text drives
home his meaning: "*Now* is the accepted time . . . *now*
is the day of salvation."

The impact of biblical time at every point in history
is to face man with inescapable decision. Measured
time, as in Ecclesiastes, by picturing everything as having "a season and a time" thinks to avoid the decision
of *now* by escape into the round of nature. But this is
illusion. The seasons return, it is true, but we are never
the same. Whitehead, the philosopher, put it strikingly
when he declared that the only possible place of meeting for the communion of saints is in the "insistent
present." He who dallies with time, lacking in serious-
ness about the present moment, not only loses his ren-
dezvous with destiny but also fails to see that eternal
life is cradled in the "now." And to miss the redeeming
significance of either grace or judgment in this moment
is to turn irretrievably in upon oneself. Apart from
kairos the perfectly sensible but equally self-deluded
crook in Auden's play, "For the Time Being" is right
in congratulating himself upon hearing the news of the
Christ child. "I like committing crimes," he reasons.
"God likes forgiving them. Really the world is ad-
mirably arranged!"

Begin now to walk in the Spirit. Consider, second,
the word *walk.* In Ephesians 4:1, Paul uses this expression again: "I therefore, the prisoner of the Lord, be-
seech you that ye walk worthy of the vocation
wherewith ye have been called, with all lowliness and
meekness, with longsuffering, forbearing one another

in love; endeavoring to keep the unity of the Spirit in the bond of peace." Many of us would hold back by saying, "Oh, but I don't have that kind of faith." Let me suggest that you walk for one week, one day—even one hour—as if you did have that kind of faith. Try it and see what happens. Someone has said that if God bores you, tell him about it in prayer. Let us add, if God frightens you with his demands, try fulfilling them in all earnestness. At worst you will have some reason for complaint; more likely, you will come to know a deeper meaning of Christ's assurance that his yoke is easy if borne in faith and trust.

Faith is commitment *in via*. It is not assent *in vacuo*. Then to walk by faith is to know a strength of grace denied those who complain from the sidelines. I am comforted by the fact that the lepers who sought healing from Christ, were sent off to the Temple, and they were cured while they went in the way! To walk in the Spirit is to walk in freedom knowing the immediacy of God to every need. It is to make the petition, "Give us this day our daily bread," a charter for living. It is to discover response and love hitherto untapped in the depths of your being. Habit, guarded by fear, is the self-imposed prisonhouse of our existence. Only animals can live entirely by habit. But he who ventures in faith to walk by the Spirit has already recovered something of his humanity in relation to the source of all personhood. Look, then, on Christ and find yourself as found in him—as you walk by the Spirit.

Finally, our walking is *in the Spirit*. We have this promise: "If any man be in the Spirit he is a new creation." To walk by the Spirit is to yield one's life fully in the obedience of faith; it means to come under the sway of the Spirit, it is to live in the church where the Spirit may have its way with us. Paul has said, "No man can call Jesus Lord save by the Holy Spirit." I take this to mean that no man can call him "Lord" save in such a way as to know for himself that he has come into the presence and the power of *his* Lord and *his* Christ. In that moment of knowing, all barriers fall away and one is *in* Christ as Peter was *in* Christ when he confessed Jesus to be the Messiah. From this moment onward, he who spoke previously from the outside now sustains and leads from within. Obedience in faith, then, becomes a kind of hearing of God's word which has the power to transform and transfigure our lives.

We walk by faith, not by sight. It is not simply that God has done certain things in the past. He is at work in us now—redeeming the time, transfiguring our lives after his own fashion as we commit ourselves to walk by the Spirit. We are confronted not only by an inescapable decision in the person of Christ but also by grace. The significance of Christ is that grace, which is the end and purpose of history, now dwells in our midst. So Augustine was able to assure his own generation with words which should prove to be a source of strength for us:

> Look not for any way except himself by which to come to him. For if he had not vouchsafed to be the way we should all have gone astray. Therefore he became the way by which thou shouldest come. I do not say to thee, "Seek the way." The way itself is come to thee: arise and walk.[5]

• *Notes for Chapter 14*

1. Galatians 5:25.
2. II Corinthians 6:2b.
3. II Corinthians 6:4 and 10 (KJV).
4. See I Peter 1:4 (Ronald Knox translation).
5. From *An Augustine Synthesis,* arranged by Erich Przywana (New York: Sheed & Ward, Inc., 1936).

15: The Person and Truth

Jesus said to him, "I am the way, and the truth, and the life; no one comes to the Father, but by me." [1]

GOETHE has said that one is never satisfied with a portrait of a person he knows. This or that feature is distorted, the expression is never quite exact, something always remains unsaid. Is the reason, perhaps, that every symbol of the person is never more than a rough approximation? In the translation by James Moffatt of the text above, the words of Jesus are rendered, "I am the real and living way. . . . If you knew me, you would know my father too."

If we *only* knew! Who is able to know another? Who, for that matter, really knows himself? It is said that Jesus "knew what was in man." [2] Add to that witness the fact that through obedience he emptied himself and was found in fashion like man, and the direction of our self-knowledge becomes somewhat clearer. It is discovered neither in ourselves, nor in our vain efforts to catalogue and imitate others, but straight ahead in the person of Jesus Christ; for here it is revealed that the steadfast love of God which is new every morning is the personal foundation of our very being. "Nothing," wrote Meister Eckhardt, "is so near to the being, so intimate to them than being itself. But God is being-itself." To become a person then in the deepest sense is to embody the counterpart of that grace and truth which was found in Jesus Christ. It is to find oneself in him.

CHRIST ON OUR DOORSTEPS

But you may object, "I do not find myself in Christ. He belongs to a world of stained-glass windows and of a Bible with 'thee's' and 'thou's.' I live in a world of brutal reality where things are never so smooth; it's about all I can do to keep from throttling those whom I am supposed to love." Perhaps this is only what we would say if we had the courage to speak the truth. But if it is true that Christ came to save not the righteous but the sinners, it's high time we sinners recognized him wherever he appears—outside as well as in the church.

If the New Testament is to be trusted, Christ is always invading hell in order to preach the gospel. That means that he is on our doorsteps too. One apt description of hell is that it is that condition in which people are not able to love any more. Loveless men and women stagger through life hoping to find what they cannot give in marriage, in children, in work without zest, and in play without abandonment. Behind the hell of not being able to give or to receive love is the gnawing pain that there is nothing real about us to give—we are mere figures on a stage who dance and strut through scenes that end with a titter or a sigh.

We are not the first people to feel this sense of noth-ingness. It must have prompted the question of one of the ancient Psalmists:

> O Lord, what is man that thou dost regard him,
>   Or the son of man that thou doest think of him,
> Man is like a breath,
>   His days are like a passing shadow.[3]

But is man "a thing of nought" as one of the older translations puts it? Is this the same creature as the one animal who is willing to die for truth? Where is the one whom God created in the beginning and "left him in the power of his own inclination"? [4]

WE ARE BECAUSE GOD IS

The foundation of reality for us, the basis of truth and of our personhood, rests in knowing that God is the source of our being. He *is* and we *are*—only through him. Our sufficiency is of God. The one thing which always seems to be excluded in our massive educational system is education in our own littleness and ignorance. Socrates may have been puzzled by the saying of the Delphic Oracle that "no man in Athens was wiser than he," but few modern graduates would seem to be both-ered by a similar estimate of their wisdom. And Soc-rates' ironic solution to this mystery—namely, that to know that one knows nothing is a high degree of knowl-edge—would hardly have occurred to most of us be-cause we have never encountered such an idea in our schools where knowledge is for power and control. Power is heady stuff and those who drink its cup are not prone to remember their littleness nor God's greatness. But our renewing as persons begins just there. We recover something of this conviction each time we sing the *Jubilate Deo:*

> Be ye sure that the Lord he is God;
> It is He that hath made us and not we ourselves;
> We are his people, and the sheep of his pasture.

A man knows himself in a primary way in relation to that which *is*—the abiding reality which endures. In biblical terms our identity always refers back to God. Because he *is*, we *are*. It is here also that biblical religion meets and rejects the notion born of pride that the self possesses absolute autonomy. The self does not stand alone. Its existence depends upon self-giving in response to love, rather than in self-withholding as a way of protecting an autonomous territory. The truth of the gospel remains: We have a self only as we spend it in love.

THE TRUTH THAT IS LIVING TRUTH

But others would begin their definitions of truth elsewhere. Most would agree that truth has something to do with conforming to reality. Then the problem of defining reality faces us. One tradition, the Pythagorean, held that all things are comprehended in number. All things may be counted, they held. Hence, truth is number. Obviously it is true that all things may be counted, but this is not all that may be said. William

Temple was fond of the saying that while numbers tell
us something about everything they tell us little about
anything. Perhaps you prefer the poet's definition:

> Beauty is truth, truth beauty—that is all
> Ye know on earth, and all ye need to know.[5]

Even if we grant the proposition of some of the
philosophers that every multiplication table already
implies a relation to God—that is, we cannot count at all
without the implicit assumption of infinity—yet this is
not the God of faith nor the living truth. The biblical
assumption is that truth is personal and that reality is
rooted in personality. Any abstraction, whether of number or of doctrinal formula, is but a fraction of truth;
living truth is known only in personal relation. In Christ
there is no escape from the personal encounter with
truth. In him the word of truth becomes living flesh and
no man comes to the Father, that is, to ultimate reality,
unless he is willing to meet truth in person. Here truth
is tested and proved not by argument but in witness and
in action. There is a place in biblical religion for the
testing and proving of *beliefs about God* by logic, but
it does not belong to the primary area of knowing and
of actively responding to the living truth in God.

Jesus said, "I am the truth." If "the style is the man
himself" as we say, then, the style of Jesus as Christ tells
us something of what it really means to be a person and
to know and become truth. For the eyes that see and
the ears that hear, a mode of life tends to say as much
about the meaning of that life as the words which attempt to explain it. There is one condition: our hearing
must be with faith,[6] with loving response. Paul Tournier

in his book, *The Meaning of Persons,* tells of a tuber-
culosis sanitarium in Switzerland where the doctors
were helped significantly in their care of patients by
observing the costumes which their charges chose for
a masquerade ball. No doubt they *heard* not only with
the technical understanding of medicine but also *with
faith* in the sense that we are using the expression.

We get some idea of what the early Christians *heard*
in Jesus Christ, as it is reflected in Paul's brief summary
in Romans 8:15, "For you did not receive the spirit of
slavery to fall back into fear, but you have received the
spirit of sonship." As living truth, Christ walked by the
Spirit in such a way as to banish fear and to bestow
freedom and sonship upon those who heard him with
faith. In like manner the predominant style of Christianity in history has been one of delivering men from
fear and of firing them with the promise that all men
are to become Sons of God. In this light the masks
which we assume, the "phony" personages behind
which we hide, are but one more evidence that we refuse to hear the freedom-bestowing word in Christ, but
prefer our old ways of fear and manipulation to genuine
meeting.

The Fourth Gospel is packed with this theme.
Throughout it man is pictured as encountering the living truth in Christ. Nicodemus, the woman at the well,
the wedding guests at Cana were all like Jacob in the
desert night—close enough in that place to reach out
and touch living truth *and they knew it not!* But, even
so, the catastrophic meaning of their encounter finally
struck home. What happens to the many who, like
Pilate, also brush against that presence but are so locked

in the boredom and jaded trance of their own self that they can only mutter irritatedly, "What is truth"?

TO BE A PERSON

To be a person is to be alive in truth, to be in relation and in touch with truth. It is to know God as his sons, and not as alien—and thus to know others as brothers rather than as enemies. Freedom is the effectual mode of the person—freedom *from* fear and *for* becoming what we potentially already are. Is this the character of our relation with others? Is it not rather that our one great drive is not for a mutual relationship but for power over others? We want to impress them, obligate them, even possess them, but hardly ever to give ourselves to them in genuine exchange. Kierkegaard has said that for him one of the greatest proofs that God is God and that man is *not* God is that God can have a relationship to man which affords the full freedom of man. But man can never help another without at the same time making the other dependent on him—a dependency which becomes a ready tool for manipulation.

The person is never a finished product. He is open to change in every moment of his being and becoming. He lives not by mere survival—except in catastrophe—but by faith and the relationships of trust which permit him to live into the image of himself reflected in love from beyond himself. It is this aspect of continual shaping and refashioning *in via* that distinguishes man's personhood. He is a pilgrim, and, like the Mayflower Pilgrims, his being is renewed as he sees himself and his neighbors as "God's free people" on the way to becoming God's covenanted people.

To be a person, then, requires the exercise of voluntary commitment and a willingness to accept responsibility from the hands of God. Involuntary authority has increasingly become the mark of this era of history. The totalitarian states have decided that security is more essential than freedom. Their plea is that they are giving man what he wants. Certainly there are many Americans who regard the extension of freedom and civil liberties as dangerous. They, too, think that they know what is best for man. But the voluntary acceptance of authority and obedience to the same in freedom are among the inalterable conditions of personhood. No individual can long remain a person if these privileges are denied or undermined. Slavery, like freedom, is first of all a state of mind which takes root in the heart and becomes the habit of the whole man.

The quality of our personhood is rooted in the loyalties embodied in the truth or the falsehood of lives. For the Christian that loyalty begins in the discovery of an identity which belongs to his relation to God. He who claims himself in Christ finds himself a forgiven self. Forgiveness is the concrete experience of that newness of being which is possible within Christianity. The person who knows himself to be the object of that love which endures all things is thereby enabled to open himself to truth at every level, knowing that "the way, the truth, and the life" have already come to him.

• *Notes for Chapter 15*

1. John 14:6.
2. John 2:25.
3. Psalm 144:3,4.
4. Sirach 15:14.
5. John Keats, in "Ode on a Grecian Urn."
6. Galatians 3:2 and Romans 10.

16: Freedom: The Mode of the Person

> ✍ If you continue in my word, you are truly my disciples, and you will know the truth, and the truth will make you free.[1]

IN A LETTER written to his beloved brother Theo in April, 1890, Vincent Van Gogh spoke of his work and of his most recent ordeal in a series of mental depressions. His last canvas, he wrote, had been painted "with calm and a great firmness of touch. And the next day," he continued, "down like a brute. Difficult to understand things like that, but alas it's like that." The artist counseled his brother not to grieve for him but rather to run his household well—that would encourage and sustain Vincent in dark days. "Then, after a time of affliction," he concluded, "perhaps peaceful days will come again." When one reads these words one catches a glimpse of that irrepressible freedom and beauty of spirit which Van Gogh translated onto canvas. His mastery of brush and paint touch the living truth for all to behold and to be made free and whole again.

Is not this the manner of our freedom in Christ? We are persons after the mode of heaven, and freedom is the mode of heaven—where for the joy that is set before us every cross is endured in hope. Freedom is also the mode of the person. It is that mark of maturity—that transcendence of spirit—which has endured every temptation to sell the soul for small gain or to be broken by adversity. Paul, as a person and as free, sounds the note of our personhood when he declares, "If God is for us, who is against us?" [2] Behind the conviction of Paul there are the acts of God in human history—saving events—which reveal a heart set upon us in love from the beginning which will not forsake nor be deterred until we are all gathered in an eternal Kingdom. As we abide in that promise—and walk by its light—we shall know the truth which makes us free.

But what is the destiny or dignity of this creature fashioned for freedom in a civilization which, as Lewis Mumford has said, "gives power to the machines that are almost human and takes away power, initiative, and autonomy from human beings who become thereby almost machines"? What happens to freedom and the person when "medicated survival" becomes more important than living, and tinseled happiness the goal of so many? Surely the absence of joy in contemporary life is some measure of our lost contact with reality, for joy is always born out of the fulfillment which comes with the union of person and truth. It is not found by avoiding pain or by hiding a grimace behind a bland smile. Joy is the truth of God breaking into the world at a point where it has lain too long in sin and sorrow. It is, as a poet has put it, "the grace we say to God."

THE LINGERING MEMORY

Man is the creature who must live with some purpose in order to survive. He is always remembering and searching breathlessly for that "lost lane-end into heaven." It is said that Alexander Woollcott complained bitterly in his last illness: "Doctors want to keep me alive," he said, "but I want to live!" Remaining alive and *living* are two different things for any person outside a concentration camp. Why? Perhaps it is because there is within us a faint memory of something we were to become, some far-off Jerusalem that will not let us forget. Perhaps even more poignantly, it is because we know in the vernacular of the day that "we are not what we are cracked up to be." G. K. Chesterton used to say that he was often moved to frivolity in answer to the questions which were put to him in the catechism, "What are you?" and "What then is the meaning of the fall of man?" In answer to the first he was often tempted to say, somewhat irreverently, "God only knows!" But then he was sobered and checked by that second question. It means, he thought, "that whatever I am I am not myself." Here is inescapable truth: in order to discover himself and his freedom man must first face the fact that he is not himself.

If God is the One to whom "all hearts are open, all desires known" then surely man was meant for more than a self-contained existence. In order to be himself he must know himself in relation to God—and to others. There is in the book of Ezekiel that passage of consummate beauty cited before, which reveals this lost integrity of man. It is a funeral dirge over the King of

Tyre—a lamentation for an almost realized perfection,

> Thou sealest up the sum, full of wisdom, and
>   perfect in beauty. . . .
> Thou wast perfect in thy ways from the day that
>   thou wast created, till iniquity was found in thee.
> Thine heart was lifted up because of thy
>   beauty, thou hast corrupted thy wisdom by reason
>   of thy brightness. . . .[3]

Man is a creature who corrupts his wisdom by his pride and destroys his beauty by iniquity from within. His freedom becomes, rather than a *Te Deum* of praise and thanksgiving, the cloak behind which he hides his inordinate and intemperate claims. He is not himself. He is anything but himself—one who dares not trust himself to real living, one who clings to the fringes of mere survival, ingloriously enslaved in petty habits, insidious prejudices, and abysmal fear. This is the same creature who was meant to be *the very seal of perfection!*

MAN WAS FASHIONED FOR FREEDOM

But God does not give up. He who fashioned the heart of man—who understands all his works—knows also that the crucial problem for man lies beyond mere survival, in the human will and its devotions. Indeed, the meaning of Jesus Christ is just this: that God in Jesus Christ *knew what is in man* and still he does not turn from his intention to claim us for his own. Grace means God does not suffer us to be abandoned. Here is the solid foundation of freedom and personal integrity. If God be for us—even in our apostacy to freedom—who (ourselves included) can be against us? Here it is clear that the soul of freedom is more than the removal of restrictions, more than *laissez-faire* economics! It is even more than freedom *from* the whole system of trying to prove our worth (increasingly conceived in a technical society as some impersonal commodity or service). Freedom is rather an enablement— freedom for that self-consummation and mastery over the earth intended from the beginning. In freedom man finds himself *under* grace rather than *under* law. It is the mode of his response to the prior grace and freedom of God.

Freedom, then, as the mode of the person, is a sign of the new order in which God has set man beyond his slavery to sin. It is an expression of the New Being— newness of life—at work in the world. It is *God with us* wrestling with the enslaving powers and enabling man to come into his own inheritance *under* grace, for though freedom belongs to man in his depths it is not an inherited capacity. It must be appropriated by each individual in faith. It must be received as a gift. To be sure, freedom is *both* the gift and the goal of our life together. Still no man (or nation) wins freedom apart from the soul-searching revelation that all is given.

Every child knows the meaning of freedom as gift. They live in terms of immediate realities—where all the world is gift—sometimes to the acute embarrassment of adults! Like the mother in the popular Broadway play, "Mrs. McThing," parents are always discovering that children will not be fenced-in by protective walls and fierce sentiments of possessiveness. Children know that beyond the barriers set by parents in their passion to "keep things as they are" a new world of excitement beckons to them—for the poor little rich boy, the world of "Dirty Eddie's" saloon. Similarly the child "knows" love and faith long before he knows any of the facts about the world. It is here in the freedom and givenness of these familiar relationships that one is able to grow toward maturity and the giving of these gifts in return.

It is said that habit is second nature. Is freedom then our *first* nature, that is, the character of life prior to the fall? Habit, in securing our mechanical action, does not belong to the deeper realm of response. Further, freedom and the person are inconceivable apart from response. Perhaps we may say that habit is represented in the masks we wear—our "personage" as contrasted with our genuine person. If real meeting is to take place between persons it is obvious that some penetration behind these screens must take place. It is interesting that Luther referred to all creatures as "masks of God." The Divine is hidden behind that which is apparent. When the veil is torn away most people fear that they will be revealed as naked and inexcusable. In the light of the gospel the opposite is true: the unmasking which took place once and for all in the Cross reveals the infinities of our unguessed goodness in Christ. There we come to the courage to face ourselves because there we learn the secret of God's love—that he looks upon us only as found in Christ.

The new revolution which Christianity has wrought is just this: it has made freedom, like truth, a living reality—a personal quality—meaningless apart from freedom in the person. And it has rooted this new birth of freedom forever in the work of Christ.

THE MARK OF THE FREE PERSON

What are the distinguishing marks of the person in freedom? Certainly one of the first is his personal integrity and identity. The age-old faith of the Hebrews, "Hear, O Israel: the Lord our God is one Lord," [4] has introduced this note of integrity into our spiritual bloodstream. God's oneness is the precondition of our oneness. Apart from that oneness where we drift in a world that has banished God but not its guilt; we are torn asunder by our ambivalences; and, like the fleeing Jonah in Father Mapple's sermon, we dread most of all that "macerating" question, "Who's there?" Identity rests upon the sure foundation of one's relationship with that which endures. For the Hebrew, names were crucially important; they not only pointed to the uniqueness of the person, but also to his fundamental identity in Yahweh. To use a personal name carelessly was and is an abomination in the Hebrew community. It is well remembered that Jacob wrestled in the night with an unknown assailant and that his curiosity (or idolatry?) went unrewarded—even rebuffed: "Wherefore is it that thou dost ask after my name!" [5]

The surest sign of well-grounded identity is the capacity to *see* and *hear* another. He who has a self to give is able to lose it in listening to another. And listening with response restores all the freshness and wonder of new creation. This is the way the world is made new. The soul that waits in readiness to hear bears the seal of the person. He who hears us in our inmost depths is none other than God himself—and we who are called by his name find ourselves in listening.

The mode of freedom is also marked by the assumption of responsibility—by self-direction and personal choice. Belief in God is an occasion *not* for infantile dependency but for responsible freedom. If perfect love casts out fear, it is only those who have *not* been made perfect in love—the anxiety-ridden and the guilt driven who *use* "religion" as an escape from responsible freedom. Though every act of free choice involves the inescapable passage through the gate of anxiety, God's grace is sufficient in faith. Still it is remarkable how much of the Bible is concerned with man's effort to escape from his own freedom and to reduce God to a kind of divine "Mr. Fix-It"! But just as Yahweh refused Moses, and Jesus his disciples, so God will not take over our freedom by acts of divine fiat. The mode of freedom in the person is a life made up of "agonizing reappraisals." There can be no automation in freedom.

FROM RELIGION TO FAITH

It is just here in its insistence upon responsible freedom that Christianity makes its most radical and perhaps startling claim. Throughout the ages men have always approached the Divine with their plea, "Art thou he that should come or do we look for another?" Christ not only frustrated their eagerness for a magic sign by pointing to the healing power of the Kingdom already in their midst, but actually diverted their attention *from religion to faith.* The inevitable tendency of all religion is to institutionalize man's idolatry. The full implications of the Hebraic belief that neither heaven nor earth can contain Yahweh are manifest in Christ's refusal to become domesticated to the folk mores of first-century Palestine. He set his face resolutely against the prudent, all-too-human claims of man and toward a self-emptying Cross outside Jerusalem. In one remarkable passage [6] the people clamored for the secret of how to do the "work of God"—no doubt impressed with his "works." "This is the work of God," he replied, "that you believe in him whom he has sent." Responsible freedom requires, *first*, response to a person and, *second*, the employment of self-direction within the confidence of that prior relationship. In Christianity, technology (how to do it) is properly kept as the servant of faith and freedom—and this proper relationship is the *Magna Carta* of the person.

If freedom is the mode of the person we cannot conclude this brief survey of its distinguishing marks without mentioning that summation of both person and freedom, namely the capacity for self-transcendence. A passionate theme and prayer for every Christian is set forth in Kierkegaard's expression: "Purity of heart is to will one thing; to be oneself in the eyes of God." *To will one thing* in the eyes of God is different from achieving a singleness of purpose, which may be found in the successful criminal; and *to will to be oneself* in the eyes of God requires something more than a round of self-congratulation. It requires the courage of self-acceptance which is grounded in something that transcends the self. Kierkegaard projected both in his chosen epitaph: "That individual."

Paradoxically the uniqueness and self-transcendence of the person in freedom are found together in the individual. But it is not the isolated "individual" nor the deluded individualists which Kierkegaard has in mind. It is to come to oneself, to discover oneself *in the eyes of God*. It is to find ourselves as found in Christ—beyond all "outer," "inward," or "other" directedness! John Oman once said with regard to the relation of *Grace and Personality:* "We stand with our faces toward our world and our backs toward ourselves and only catch fleeting glimpses of ourselves over our shoulders. . . ." [7] Perhaps it could be added that we are saved by those "fleeting glimpses"; for here Kierkegaard's prayer is at least partially fulfilled; in seeing ourselves behind our worldly front, we *see* with the eyes of God in both judgment and in grace. Kierkegaard's definition of faith put the matter with economy of words: "Faith is; that the self in being itself and in willing to be itself is grounded transparently in God."

Integrity, responsibility, and the transcending capacity to see oneself as seen in God—these are the concrete modes of man's freedom as a person. But a warning is in order. Like faith—and all the Christian "virtues"—these are the assurances we live by—"the conviction of things not seen." The Christian lives by promises and participation—not as the finished product of some process. His characteristic posture is one of forgiving and being forgiven, within the community of faith. His prayer is set forth in the collect for the Eleventh Sunday after Trinity [8]: ". . . That we running to Thy promises, may be made partakers of Thy heavenly treasure. . . ."

• *Notes for Chapter 16*

1. John 8:31-32.
2. Romans 8:31.
3. Ezekiel 28:12,15,17 (KJV).
4. Deuteronomy 6:4.
5. Genesis 32:29 (KJV).
6. John 6:25-34.
7. John Oman, *Grace and Personality* (Cambridge, England: Cambridge University Press, 1931, 4th ed.), p. 46.
8. With slight alteration suggested by Massey Shepherd.

17: Fashioned in Grace

In one of his entertaining essays, "The Colloid and the Crystal," [2] Joseph Wood Krutch compares the amoeba and the snowflake. The amoeba, being the simplest form of organic life, presents an unspectacular appearance, a shapeless particle under the magnifying glass. The crystalline snowflake on the other hand is a dazzling mass of angles and reflected color. *But,* it is pointed out, this undistinguished jelly called the amoeba bears a promise not for itself alone but for mankind as well; while the snowflake, for all its beauty, holds nothing more than the fixed arrangement of water, light, and color. "After the passage of billions of years," writes Krutch, "one can see and hear the other, but their relationship can never be reciprocal." No combination of organic cells is ever likely to achieve the effortless beauty of the crystal on the first day of creation, but organic life as called forth in the person "can know as the crystal cannot know, what beauty is."

We are persons set in a world of crystalline beauty,

intended for dominion and fashioned in grace. We are persons who alternately grab for and weep over the beauty and perfection of the inorganic, but who sell our souls for advertising gimmicks and plunder the earth—our birthright—for ready cash.

SUCH MAGNITUDES!

Whether or not we like it we cannot exchange places with the structured beauty of the snowflake. We are born to be persons in relation to one another and to the ultimate Person. Our achievements are meager when all is said and done, beside the timeless monuments of nature. Hart Crane may have reason enough to break into lyric praise at the sight of the arched span of the George Washington Bridge. But, silence alone is adequate to convey that inexpressible wonder which is ours on almost any starry night as we behold the scene laid before us. Like some immortal Isaiah we are witnessess as the Shepherd of the stars calls them one by one to take their place among the heavenly hosts—the spiral galaxy of the middle heavens, Arcturus, Orion, and the Pleiades.

To behold ourselves in relation to such magnitudes is to come again to the proper relationship, not only as between the colloid and the crystal—between the living person and the silent world—but also to the proper relation between man and God. Unfortunately the magnitudes are increasingly shut out of our artificially lighted civilization. Unlike the ancient psalmist who found comfort in the enduring presence of God against his own transience, modern man becomes obsessed with his days which are gone like a shadow and withered like grass. He finds no comfort in the clean and purifying fear of the Lord, which for the Hebrew drove out all lesser fear and self-centered concern. In short, modern man envies the sure seasons of nature. The grass turns green again, the seasons come and go, the stars run their appointed course. Only man painfully counts the days. He alone weeps for his spent youth and trembles before his anticipated demise. No wonder he develops a penchant for numbering things! Behind all this feverish counting in our technological world there is, surely, a deep-seated covetousness for the unchanging rhythms of nature and the lifeless beauty of the crystal. Is this not simply another way of saying that in such a world, where love is so rare, the lifeless formula is preferred to the risks of life and death? It is sobering to remember that it was said of the damned in Dante's classic: "These have no hope of death."

But God will not let us go! Nor can the sterile beauty of the inorganic be ours. In order to become beauty in his own way man must find meaning in his personal relations. The word *growth* is supreme in nature, that is to say, *growth* and *process*—but man cannot become himself unless he knows something more, namely, the love of a person. Human history is the story of man's love, such as it is, writ large in the imagination of his heart. That his "time" is fulfilled partly by growth—by *becoming* in the organic sense—only qualifies in a specific way the manner of his being shaped by his deepest loves.

GRACE IS PERSONAL

We are fashioned in grace—and grace is entirely personal. Biblical history is an impressive witness to the character of God as faithfulness and abiding grace. The first Christians lived with the knowledge that they were fashioned in this grace. It was *there,* in their common life—in the glad and simple hearts who responded and in the *charismatta*—the gift of the Spirit, namely, love, joy, peace, good temper, kindliness, generosity, fidelity, and self-control. It was *there* in the abiding Christ. It is not without significance that the passage from Philippians just preceding our text is the widely chosen selection in the Church which is read on Palm Sunday. From that perspective—with Golgotha and Resurrection straight ahead—the faithful recall their own identity in Christ, who being the "express image" of God, emptied himself and was found in fashion as a man—one who became obedient even unto death—in order that love in person might triumph over the worst that man can do. Having recalled their identity in Christ, the *laos* (God's people) proceed to work out their salvation with "fear and trembling," as the King James Version puts it, "for it is Christ which worketh in you both to will and to do of his good pleasure."

The preparation for the receiving of such grace is bound up in our painful and slow education that nothing short of such personally effective grace can save us. When all our mechanical gadgets have finally convinced us that we are, indeed, automatons, we may be ready for grace. As a very young man G. K. Chesterton wrote these prophetic lines:

I live in an age of varied powers and knowledge,
Of steam, science, democracy, journalism, art;
But when my love rises like a sea,
I have to go back to an obscure tribe and a
   slain man
To formulate a blessing.[3]

To will and to do! Here is the short-circuit in our network of living. We *will* to be righteous, but our concern with the prestige of our righteousness leaves little room for grace. We *will* to be loving, but we put a price on our love and surround it with such conditions that we can never love or be loved. We *will* to do the truth, but our own divided heart will not yield to the cost of truth. Between our *willing* and our *doing* there is a chasm of anxious self-concern. The meaning of Christ is that this chasm has been closed by none other than God himself. What does it mean that God works in us "both to will and to do of his good pleasure"? It means as Paul has put it elsewhere [4] that Christ was made "to be sin who knew no sin, so that in him we might become the righteousness of God." If this be true, is there any place—even the dark regions of our shame—where Christ has not preceded us in love?

Here is magnitude juxtaposed to our impotence. The same Lord who knew no sin and yet became sin for us, enters into our gracelessness and becomes grace in us. He precedes us in grace. We encounter grace, that is, the presence of God, first of all while we are yet in sin. This is our own *parousia*, the future entering into us now, to use Rilke's expression, and transforming us before it happens. Christ is the *parousia* of grace whose once-and-for-all entry into time becomes in the same moment the goal of time, bending history toward an appointed meeting between God and man.

So Christ comes to every man: sometimes in love, sometimes in judgment, always in grace—most frequently in surprise. Whether to a Jacob in the desert night or to shepherds keeping their flock by night, his coming is an occasion which shakes the foundations. Browning reached out to trace such moments with the artistry of the poet when he wrote:

> Just when we're safest, there's a sunset touch,
> A fancy from a flower bell, someone's death,
> A chorus-ending from Euripides,
> And that's enough for fifty hopes and fears,
> As old and new at once as nature's self,
> To rap and knock and enter our soul,
> Take hands and dance there a fantastic ring,
> Round the ancient idol, on his base again,
> The grand perhaps! [5]

These are apt to be moments when we flee from the self-exposure of genuine meeting, when we seek the safety of law and moralism. To fall into the hands of the living God, to pass through judgment is never anything less than travail. But it is a travail of joy as well as of pain. The pain of self-exposure may be endured if we live in the assurance of the new person who is in birth. As Luther has reminded us, the law has its appointed time which is properly to bring us to an awareness of that chasm between *to will* and *to do*. But grace is eternal. "Just when we're safest," we are struck by grace, by the unguessed and eternal goodness of God.

There is more to grace than a disturbing Presence; there is personal will. Part of the astonishment of stumbling into the Presence of God is the sudden awareness that we have met before! God is no stranger to the heart. For every man there is a familiar sound in the words of Yahweh to Jeremiah, "Before I formed you in the womb I knew you." [6] We have been shaped and formed by the steadfastness of God. We have been saved again and again by his compassion which is "new every morning." This is the substance of grace, this steadfastness and this compassion. In grace therefore the personal, living, and renewing character of God's activity is foremost.

In grace we are summoned as persons in the sense that only we can give consent to him who calls. To be found of God means, we have said, to be found in sin. Even more, it is a disturbing moment of self-exposure. But one cannot escape or forfeit his freedom in this moment. It is precisely in our freedom that God summons us. The burden of grace is the freedom of the person who in deeply personal ways responds to the gift of God—always as for-giveness. To be found of God in forgiveness is to find oneself. Both the coming to oneself and the giving of oneself are made possible within the riches of God's grace.

FASHIONED IN GRACE

We are fashioned in grace. We are God's own craftsmanship—knit together in love as in our mother's womb. The form of that craftsmanship is recovered in freedom and in thanksgiving. He who finds himself new every morning, and in that new birth of freedom lives by love and thanksgiving, is transfigured daily until Christ be formed within. His is a life forever renewed from grace to faith and from faith to obedience in love. This is the root of our identity and our imperturbability—even in death, for whether we live or die we are the Lord's.

Grace, then is a time of *metanonia,* of repentance, of being turned—sometimes with a rude shock, sometimes by love that has overtaken us, always by the surprise of gift. Man is known by the things he *remembers.* For many that remembrance is only the bitter tears of the Lord's song in a foreign land. Others, having recovered the secret of their fashioning in grace, respond in the manner of Charles Williams who, we recall, declared that "repentance is no more than a passionate intention to know all things after the mode of heaven"—which is to know all things as gift, as occasions of great joy.

• *Notes for Chapter 17*

1. Philippians 2:12.
2. In *The Best of Two Worlds* (New York: William Sloane Associates, 1950).
3. From pages 7, 8 of *Paradox in Chesterton* by Hugh Kenner, copyright 1947, Sheed & Ward, Inc., New York.
4. II Corinthians 5:21.
5. In "Bishop Bloughram's Apology," *The Complete Poetic and Dramatic Works of Robert Browning,* Cambridge Edition (Boston and New York: Houghton Mifflin Company, 1895), p. 351.
6. Jeremiah 1:5.